The Self-Learning Blueprint:
A Strategic Plan to Break Down Complex Topics, Comprehend Deeply, and Teach Yourself Anything

By Peter Hollins,
Author and Researcher at
peterhollins.com

Table of Contents

Chapter 1: A Self-Learning Plan

Imagine you're starting a business. You've found a great product, and you're certain the market is going to go crazy for it. All your friends have agreed that they would *definitely* buy your product. Even better, a Google search shows that no one else has had the idea to sell this particular product. You're going to be *rich*. You start browsing private yachts online. The same friends say that you are being *premature*, but you don't know what that word means so you ignore them.

Excited by the opportunity, you build a website, buy loads of your product to keep up with your predicted demand, and prepare to ship your goods to customers. All you need to do now is buy some advertisements and wait for the orders to roll in. Business is *easy*—why don't more people start their own company?

But of course, things take a wayward turn. You are shocked to see your website advertising costs far exceed your income. Every month you are losing money, and you have made only one sale. That sale was later returned for a refund. There was never any demand for your product, your friends lied to you to be nice, and the product itself was ludicrous.

Why did you find yourself in this position, and could it have been prevented?

Proficient businessmen don't just come up with a great idea and cash in. They study and learn far before ever taking action, and when they do take action, they act in ways they know will produce the profit they seek. The failure here wasn't just one of marketing or website design; it was a failure to understand the process of self-learning and how it contributes to anything novel or new in your life. This was a high stakes situation with a lot of investment, and you set yourself up for failure by not taking the initiative to self-learn. In reality, the ability to teach yourself both simple and complex information is the silent determinant of whether you ever get from Point A to Point B.

Sadly, it's often only *after* failure does it occur to look to mentors, classes, books, or even podcasts to determine what we do wrong and how we can succeed next time. With business people, this lets them learn to analyze markets, giving them a fair idea of whether their product will be met with open arms or ignored entirely. They also learn about different methods of advertising, allowing them to reach exactly the niches they need for their product to take off. Imagine if you had understood this to be part of the process *before* you opened your wallet and flushed money down the toilet. Of course, learning on the job and in the moment is also fine, but the skill of *learning* still must be cultivated.

Now imagine another scenario—you're learning to play guitar. You don't want to be a rockstar, but playing some songs around a fire on camping trips with your kids sounds like a fun way to bond and pass the time. You pick up a guitar, spend some time strumming, and are amazed by the cacophony that can emanate from a single relatively small stringed instrument. After thoroughly annoying the family you're trying to please, you decide that you need some help.

After considering your budget and the time you have available to learn, you decide that YouTube videos and websites are the best way to learn. You set aside twenty minutes after dinner as learning time, and devote yourself to understanding chords and strumming techniques. You make sure to understand the scales and theories before delving into more complex songs.

In no time at all, you can read music well enough to play campfire songs and even add in some new riffs of your own. Because you set aside time and properly expended the effort needed to learn something new, you gained the ability to amuse yourself and entertain your friends and family. There are considerably lower stakes here, and yet, far different results.

In both examples, the key to success was the arduous process of self-learning. It can feel tedious or even impossible because you will have no idea where to start. But this stage of discomfort and confusion must be traversed for anything new in your life. You can consult experts and learn from instructional materials. You can also create your own curriculum based on the knowledge gap between where you currently are and where you want to be. What matters is that by putting time and energy into acquiring new knowledge and mastering new skills, you can get to exactly where you want to be. And once you're there, new doors will open as well.

Both of our examples produced a profit— one was monetary, and the other was social, but both acts of learning led to a net increase in quality of life for the learners. All it took was time, effort, and the willingness to apply the knowledge gleaned from expert sources.

Self-learning is what unlocks our potential in every aspect of life. However, if it were an easy task, everyone would be exactly where they want to be. It's not comfortable or easy. How we learned to learn as children is rarely the best real-life approach. The prospect of creating your own strategy and plan can be overwhelming. And whoever said it was supposed to feel like you aren't working?

In addition, it turns out there are quite a few mental blocks people have surrounding self-learning that aren't even about the process itself. They begin with the various myths, which typically amount to the statement, "You need X to learn, and if X is not present, you are forever doomed." These myths keep many people from even getting started onto the path they desire. It's worth spending some time to dispel these myths so we can dive fully into learning afterwards without any reservations.

The Myth of Requirements

Many myths are empowering and serve as points of inspiration. For instance, the ancient Greek myth of Perseus slaying the snake-haired Medusa to serve as a rallying cry that the impossible is actually quite possible.

Unfortunately, that is not the case with learning. Mostly, learning myths serve to create perceived barriers—such as a certain style, a certain formula, a certain motivation, even, are necessary to effectively think and learn. From the myth of innate learning styles to the falsehood that intelligence quotient (IQ), and thus intellectual capacity, is stable throughout life, many consider themselves to be stuck where they are. None of that is true, and there are no real prerequisites besides having an intention and some self-discipline. This section is about debunking those disempowering myths and allowing yourself even the possibility to get started to learn.

Innate intelligence or talent is needed.

Can only innately intelligent people learn adequately? Are some of us just not capable of picking things up? Are we only meant for some tasks versus others?

No, no, and no. In fact, inborn talent is only a minor factor in determining learning success. *Mindset*, as it turns out, is the most significant differentiator between successful and unsuccessful learners. Studies have shown that people with a *growth mindset* who believe they can improve with time and effort fare much better than people who may have more talent but believe that that intelligence is a fixed attribute.

There are a lot of reasons for this. People who believe intelligence is fixed set up barriers to their own success. While that sounds counterintuitive, it makes more sense if you consider that innately intelligent people don't push themselves to excel because they believe it would be useless. They may start from a higher level of performance, but they are unable to diversify and rise beyond a certain point. This limits the number and type of things they can learn. Others will accept subpar performance in areas they're "just not good at," even when consulting more resources and expending more effort could easily lead to excellence in those abandoned areas of study.

By contrast, people with a growth mindset—regardless of their initial aptitude for a given subject—know that with time, effort, and proper instruction, they can master any field. They see that the world is their oyster of opportunity. Unlike people who believe their talents determine their capacities, they know that initial failure is not a reason for despair. Instead, they see failure for what it is: an opportunity for further learning and a lesson about what not to do that they aren't likely to forget.

In addition to being unafraid of failure, people with a growth mindset have shown a willingness to take more chances, which dramatically expands the types of pursuits they can learn and master. They've also been shown to progress faster while learning, probably because they're less likely to be discouraged or accept their stumbles as permanent blocks to their progress.

The fact is, growth-oriented individuals are right when they flout the common wisdom that intelligence is set at birth. Each of us learns as we age, from infancy onward. We start out by flailing in our cribs, and then learn to raise our heads and crawl. Soon, we're taking our first steps and speaking with our parents and siblings. Eventually, we're learning algebra, reading literature, and doing our own science experiments.

All of this is part of the inescapable path through human life. We begin undeveloped and unskilled, but our brains grow, evolve, and change with use—not just in childhood, but until the day we die. Each day is an opportunity to learn, be, and do more than we ever imagined possible. All we have to do is take matters into our own hands, believe in ourselves, study from the masters, and practice new skills until their successful execution becomes part of who we are.

Certain learning styles are needed.

A second pervasive myth is that we each have unique learning styles that make it easier or harder for us to learn from certain methods and in certain mediums. This myth goes on to say that each of us is mentally programmed in a different way, such that certain styles are necessary to reach our potential.

This widespread school of thought originated from the research of a psychologist named Howard Gardner, who published the book *Frames of Mind: The Theory Of Multiple Intelligences* in 1983.

Gardner outlined eight different types of intelligence: linguistic, logical-mathematical, musical, bodily-kinesthetic, spatial, interpersonal, intrapersonal, and naturalist. These intelligences don't describe individual skills, but form part of a collective. As Gardner describes in his original theory, each intelligence is a branch of a single system of acquiring knowledge. These different branches are meant to work together to facilitate different, additional approaches to teaching people new material.

Unfortunately, pop culture transformed his work into a way of differentiating between people. Journalists and other well-meaning people promoted the idea that each of us has different ways in which we are more or less intelligent, and we have different styles of intelligence or learning that we are more or less capable of performing successfully. This served to excuse students who performed poorly, and offered an alluringly easy solution: if we presented the material in a different form, they would learn more easily.

Studies on the topic have debunked this theory—*every single study on the topic*. When people were given material to learn in their preferred style, they didn't show any tendency to learn material better or more quickly. Instead, it was discovered that everyone, regardless of their preferences, learned material best when it was presented in a form that suited the material being learned.

This makes intuitive sense. While everyone is different, we aren't so different that some of us learn sports better by reading about them; that always has to be a kinesthetic aspect. Similarly, languages must be heard and read if they're going to be pronounced and written correctly.

Gardner's original theory of multiple intelligences lines up with these findings exactly. He posited that each of us used all these methods to learn, and thought that being aware of these different avenues might help teachers find more ways to communicate with every student—not just those with "learning styles" that were suited to novel approaches.

A similar, also debunked myth about learning and the brain insisted that some people were right-brained or left-brained. Left-brained people were supposed to be more logical, while right-brained people were more artistic. Many believed that because of these supposedly biological differences, people needed to learn and act in line with their own skills and limitations.

This myth arose because of some brain scans that showed different levels of activity in each hemisphere doing different activities. But more recent brain scans have showed that the brain functions as one unit in these intellectual pursuits. In reality, the brain operates in a more holistic way in all people; we all use one hundred percent of our brains on both sides of our heads, and we aren't limited to having only a logical or artistic aptitude. Many excel at both types of learning, and so can you.

Certain motivation is needed.

A third mistake people make is waiting for the motivation to learn something new to come along. They believe there must always be a light at the end of the tunnel. This, a form of waiting for inspiration to strike, is a mistake. Let's face it, no one is going to enjoy or feel some inherent motivation or desire to learn something they simply don't care about. Whether it's calculus or a new piece of software, the end goals do not always justify the means. There's no way it's always going to have an enjoyable or pleasurable element, and there's not always a silver lining.

If we take those statements to be true, it means that motivation isn't what will get you off the couch; *confidence* is.

Confidence is your belief in your ability to attain a specific goal. If you have high confidence, you believe you can accomplish the task you've set out to do. If you have low confidence, you're afraid you're going to fail in reaching your goals. High confidence drives you toward learning because you know if you stumble or fall, you'll be able to pick yourself right back up again. You know you're competent, capable, and able to finish what you start. This confidence motivates you to continue, as there's no internal friction preventing you from careening toward your goals.

By contrast, low confidence is riddled with fear and doubt. When you're not confident, you wonder what will happen if you make mistakes, and you become afraid of how many mistakes you'll make. Lacking confidence, you compare yourselves to others who have achieved your goal, and you wonder how you could ever hope to achieve that level of greatness. When you don't have confidence, every imperfection stands out like a testament to your incompetence, and it feels like finishing your project is impossible. Why even get off the couch at all, in that case?

Learning is hard work. It takes time and effort. Genuinely challenging yourself to learn new information never comes easily for anyone. There's no reason to wait around for the mood to study to strike; that mood will probably never come. Learning isn't always fun, and it isn't something you can only do when it feels good.

Learning is how we become more than we already are. It's difficult. But if you have a sense of security in what you can accomplish, then what's the holdback in getting started, besides some laziness?

A certain amount of time is needed.

Even when people know things they could learn to improve their lives, many put off that learning by claiming not to have enough time. This excuse is exacerbated by the public notion that it takes massive amounts of time to become proficient in a new skill or hobby. Avoidance of learning is actually *encouraged* by a rule of thumb popularized in Malcom Gladwell's book,

Outliers: The Story of Success. In it, Gladwell claims that it takes ten thousand hours of practice to master a new skill. With such a high benchmark for success, it's no surprise that many look at that figure and decide they're too busy to learn. After all, if failure is guaranteed by an inability to generate ten thousand hours of free time, why should someone start learning something new? In that time, you could watch hundreds of movies, go on hundreds of dates, and nap for hundreds of hours with time to spare.

Fortunately, this myth is as false as it is pervasive.

If you spend three hours shooting a bow and arrow on your own, you'd learn a little bit. But compare that time in undirected self-study to three hours spent with an expert marksman, who can watch and correct your form and better direct your focus toward the techniques you need to master. Are both sessions likely to be equally effective? Of course not. Having a teacher makes it quicker and easier to learn the skills you need and eliminate the bad habits that inevitably surface when you begin to practice any skill. (And of course, having a strategic plan combined with some self-discipline will also get you there faster than you might think.)

Gladwell's ten thousand hours completely ignores the reality that the quality of practice matters a good deal more than the quantity of practice we perform.

According to bestselling author Daniel Goleman, *deliberate practice* usually requires "someone with an expert eye" to help you identify the specific ways you can improve and to motivate you to reach your greatest heights. "Without such feedback, you don't get to the top ranks. The feedback matters and the concentration does, too— not just the hours." With expert guidance, we can eject our mistaken notions and bad habits and get to our destination in the shortest amount of time possible.

With deliberate, quality practice, we can employ special techniques and shortcuts that transform learning from a long road littered with self-reinforcing mistakes, to a shorter, easier road where mistakes are spotted early and proper techniques are mastered swiftly. When we have good guidance, whether it's in the form of a mentor or quality instructional materials, we have our attention and our practice focused, and we become more efficient learners. In brief, it really is possible to work smarter, not harder. And when we do that, we save a lot of time.

In short, the ten-thousand-hour rule is somewhat incomplete, and though learning is linear, you can certainly think smarter and not harder.

Macro and Micro Planning

Now you know that you don't need to be talented, you don't need to cater to learning styles, and you don't need boatloads of time to learn a new skill. There are no true prerequisites except perhaps a willingness to work hard.

So what is *actually* needed? Well, a plan. Specifically, two plans. Planning should be done at the macro and micro levels. At the macro level, you examine your overall goals and purposes for learning. This is where you make sure that you are spending your time the way you want to. At the micro level is when you plan out your days and hours with activities specifically suited to reaching those goals. Here, you make sure that the time you are spending yields the result that you desire.

The macro level can be accomplished by following six steps.

First, decide what you want to learn. This seems obvious, but there are better and worse things to spend your time on.

When considering a course of action, you will want to first consider your strengths and weaknesses. Often, whether it's in work or in play, we're better off emphasizing and developing our strengths than we are trying to minimize our failings. After all, no one is going to ask us to do everything, and when we really have trouble, acquiring help from others is always possible. But excellence in one area, or a small group of areas, easily transforms us into experts in our fields, which is a highly desirable place to be. Emphasizing your strengths when you choose an area to develop is a good idea. Of course, if you want to learn something totally new, that's also something you can accomplish!

Even if you're only looking to advance your professional skillset, you should still consider what you want to do when choosing a subject to learn or a skill to develop. Career paths are a consideration, but it's even more important to consider what sorts of activities make you happy and unhappy. You don't want a degree in accounting if you hate numbers, after all, even if it would improve your paycheck. Paths that align with your interests and are emotionally fulfilling are usually more rewarding.

Consider Darlene, who works as a web developer. She wants to have greater control over the processes that occur on her websites, rather than outsourcing for code when she needs it to perform certain functions she can't create herself. Moreover, she wants to be able to manipulate that code and make it from scratch so that she completely understands what's on her pages. Her vision for her learning is gaining knowledge of more types of code so that she can be a more competent, better-rounded web developer.

The second step is analyzing your current skills and experience to spot gaps in knowledge. Where are you lacking compared to your future self? What do you already know and do well? What do you still need to learn? Can other people fill in these gaps in knowledge for you, or do you need to step up to the plate and seek out additional resources? Once you find areas in which you need to improve, you will be able to discern specific areas you can study and skills you should develop to come closer to your goals. This gives your plan a concrete shape, because you will know exactly what you are missing to get to Point B.

Darlene already develops web pages for a living and knows the most current versions of HTML and CSS by heart, but she currently outsources certain types of coding to others. This leads to problems with version control and gives her a sense of powerlessness over that aspect of her job. If she wants to fill that gap in her knowledge, she needs to study other languages used on the web. She decides to start with Java, as that's the code she most often interacts with without understanding.

Third, identify the proper solution to your problem/deficiency/goal. This is about surveying your resources. Part of this will depend on your temperament. Are you a self-starter, or do you learn better in a classroom setting? Do you need a source of knowledge you can pick up and put down as your schedule allows, or can you afford to set up regular appointments with a teacher to develop a skill? Your schedule, income, and preferences all play a role in determining the right resources to seek and employ.

Lots of learning resources exist in the modern world, from books, journals, webpages, and podcasts, to seminars, work teams, and formal classes, to one-on-one instructional training in formal and informal settings.

When choosing a resource to learn from, it's important to consider your own learning preferences, but that's only one of many considerations. You must also consider the reputation of your source or teacher, and whether you will gain any formal credentials from studying with a specific teacher or demonstrating competence in a certain field. It's also essential to consider convenience, because a class you can't go to is not useful, no matter how well-regarded the teacher may be. By contrast, solo studying offers no emotional or technical support from others, while a course or a tutoring situation may involve substantial help and oversight from someone else; if this might be valuable in the area you're studying, it could be worth paying for.

Darlene is highly motivated but often pressed for time. She considers community college courses, learning from books and journals, and even hiring a private tutor, but ultimately decides to engage in one of the many online programs to help her develop her skills on her own schedule. These courses won't automatically get her credentials, but she's aware that she could take a skills test to certify herself once she gains skill mastery, and as she will have an immediate use for Java in her current job, she's not worried about being unable to use her new knowledge in the future.

The fourth step is developing your learning blueprint. Once you know what you want to accomplish, you should look for people who have already accomplished your goal. These people will serve as a step-by-step guide for how to get to where you want.

If the person is famous or no longer living, you can research their life to figure out how they became who you want to become. If they're not particularly famous or renowned, even better, as you can approach them personally and ask about their road to success. Take note of any struggles, education, or personal relationships they had to overcome or pursue to reach their goals, and try to find ways to mimic this path in your own life. This can give you deeper insight into skills to focus on and paths to pursue once your initial research project is complete.

Darlene sits down and has a conversation with her team supervisor about the best ways to advance her career and land a comparable job to her mentor when the time is right. He tells her about specific skills she'll need to learn and certifications she'll need to complete once she gains the skills she needs. He will tell her about the struggles to expect and how to overcome them. Darlene may ultimately choose a different path, but researching blueprints provides clarity and information.

The fifth step is to develop measurable goals. Your learning goals should be simple, specific, and easy to quantify. You need to set up deadlines where you will measure yourself against your expected progress using the metrics you devised, and you need to stick to that schedule. Placing your goals and expectations in a public, visible space will increase accountability by ensuring that others are aware of your project and your expectations. Remember, you should be acquiring specific, measurable skills and abilities by set points in time, and these benchmarks should all be in service of your larger learning goal.

If you've chosen a more formal environment, your class times may be set for you, but you must still set aside time to study, learn, and practice on your own time. No class gives you all the practice you need to master its skillset on the teacher's time. If you're engaging in self-study, setting up a consistent schedule for studying on your own is even more essential.

Keep in mind, genuinely mastering a skill takes a little time even with the best techniques, so be generous in the study windows you provide yourself. You don't only want time to read or watch a video, but also to reflect upon what you've learned, perform meaningful exercises, and catch and correct the errors you are inevitably going to make.

Darlene marks a schedule for herself based on the units offered in her online course, sets aside specific times to undertake each course, and allot blocks of time to study each unit. She also allocates a specific time each week to take the unit's quiz. She programs this into her phone so that she doesn't forget the plan, and prints a copy of her calendar to put on her cubicle wall. She stays on track throughout the months, and as a result, she will reach her goal of programming proficiency.

Sixth, set aside time throughout to reflect on what you're learning and reevaluate whether you're progressing at your maximum capacity. After all, if one method isn't working, that doesn't mean you're hopeless! Sometimes all you need is more accountability or greater independence to really shine. You want a learning plan that gets your skills where you want them to be, not something that isn't clicking and is therefore wasting your time. A chef will always taste their food while they are making it; you should assess your progress in a similar way.

Darlene sticks diligently to her plan and is happy with her progress, but finds the course itself a little low on support for her needs. She solves this problem by approaching her supervisor with questions when she needs further clarification. He's happy to help her along. Ultimately, she gains the skills she needs and becomes a more efficient, more skilled employee.

The macro level of a self-learning plan is not complex. In fact, it is quite simplistic. It mostly articulates a systematic process of optimizing the path you are taking.

However, at the micro level, there's still a blank. We haven't yet described the specific techniques and day-to-day activities you'll have to complete to transform learning from an idle way to pass time into a method of gaining skills that will serve you throughout your life.

Learning is the act of taking in information . . . but then what? The first step—finding a video or book and sitting down to passively absorb the information it contains—is never the problem. Even the macro plan isn't hard, and most of it will come as second nature or common sense. The hard part is transforming the knowledge we're exposed to into stable, long-term memories we can use.

What do we do with the information to truly *learn* it? How do we go from merely being able to recite *e=mc squared* to understanding how to apply it and why it works? There are four main pillars to self-learning that we will introduce here and cover throughout the book.

"Let me rephrase that . . ."

The first technique to aid learning is transforming and synthesizing information. This is simply to put new information into your own words. When we memorize verbatim, we may recall what we're taught, but we don't always have a solid grasp of what we're regurgitating. When we don't solidly grasp information, when we haven't fully integrated it into our existing knowledge, we're left with alien-sounding, unconnected factoids that are easier to forget than to remember. An example when learning an instrument is to translate the notes on the page into a visual representation of where it is on the instrument by drawing a picture or describing the placement.

By contrast, when we put information into our own words, it's rephrased in a language we intimately understand. The practice of rephrasing a concept necessitates us taking an idea into our heads, pausing to consider the essential and tertiary facts involved, and reiterating the essential and supplemental themes in new language. Rephrasing an idea requires really thinking about that idea, and concerted, conscious thought helps us remember what we've learned. Personalizing the language by making it specific to the way you speak also makes the knowledge feel more significant to you as an individual, which also helps retention. We remember what's significant to us!

"Will this be on the test?"

This refrain, parroted endlessly by students, is meant to inform students when they can stop paying attention. If it isn't on a test, the logic goes, it doesn't matter. When you're educating yourself, you can (and should!) also set up tests.

Unlike what schoolchildren believe, tests don't just exist to create a measurable grade, and they certainly aren't an end goal to reach before you can dump "useless" knowledge from your brain. They're an evaluation tool that forces you to memorize and practice the act of retrieving information from your memory. They force you to learn and recall beyond your comfort zone; just re-reading and highlighting will not get you where you want to go.

You can test yourself to gain this form of accountability and subject mastery. It doesn't only let you know what you know—and thus what you need to study—but it also helps reinforce the material you learn each time you test yourself. If you push yourself into more testing, you will not only learn the parts you find easy or intuitive, but also the facts that are more difficult and time-consuming for you to retain.

"So it's just like when Marty McFly traveled through time?"

The third pillar to help you understand and remember what you learn is linking the new knowledge to things you already know. When you create an association between two pieces of information, recalling one will help you recall the other. Instead of two discrete pieces of information that are only accessed independently, you wind up with a single, complex nexus of information, with one idea bringing the associated concept to mind automatically.

Two specific tricks that help you connect new information to existing mental models are to find analogies and create concrete examples. In both of these techniques, we require understanding to find similarities and differences between two unrelated disciplines.

"Give me some space."

Finally, the brain needs space to absorb new information. Cramming doesn't work because it's an attempt to put too much information into the brain at once. Our systems get overloaded and can't hold on to any information that way. In the end, the brain, for all the things we assign to it, is a biological thing with biological limitations.

We innately know that an athlete would need to rest between intense workouts for best performance. Take care to treat your brain the same way in the process of learning. Just because you have read X number of pages does not mean the brain will intake X pages. We cannot function properly without sleep. Even machines need to refuel and cool down. Space is required in both rest and separation from the material.

Takeaways:

- The process of self-learning is deceptively simple—that is, when you strip away all the myths surrounding it, usually amounting to prerequisites to achieve your goals.
- The myths will usually revolve around the concept of innate intelligence determining your potential, certain learning styles being necessary, certain motivations being important, or a certain predetermined rate of progress based on duration of time. These are harmful and disempowering because they tell you that you can't.
- There are no real requirements to learning other than a willingness and a dash of self-discipline. But what is massively helpful in challenging that willingness and self-discipline is a set of two plans: a macro and micro plan. The macro plan has to do with the reasons you are going to devote your time to learning something, where the micro

plan has to do with the actual activities you should engage in on a daily basis. The former ensures that you end up at a goal that you desire, while the latter ensures that you achieve that goal.

Chapter 2: The Four Pillars to Self-Learning

This is where we dig into the nitty gritty of the *micro* plan that we mentioned in the previous chapter. There are four pillars to it to focus on, but these only come into play after you complete your macro plan and understand what you're making this effort for in the first place.

Four approaches exist to transform learning from a passive and transitory experience to an activity that can impart lifelong knowledge and skills to the student. These methods are (1) transforming and synthesizing information, (2) linking concepts to your existing knowledge through examples and analogy thinking, (3) self-assessment, and (4) giving yourself space and energy for absorption. By employing these approaches to your self-study routine, you are utilizing the most powerful tools in learning all types of information.

Transform and Synthesize Knowledge

The first point of our micro plan is synthesizing information and making it our own. When we transform what we hear or read into our own words, even sometimes by simply rephrasing or summarizing things, it makes a huge difference.

There's a simpler term for transforming and synthesizing information: taking notes.

Of course, just saying it's necessary to take notes about subjects we learn about is insufficient. Most people take terrible notes, after all. Either they copy the text verbatim without giving any additional thought/insight/analysis to what was said, or they write down scrambled and highly abbreviated snippets of the original material that make the information harder to retrieve instead of easier to remember. Both methods involve a single pass through the information and completely bypass the part of notes that allows you to solidify and deepen your knowledge of the subject you're studying. There is no critical analysis or recognition that our notes become the organization for how we view a subject forever.

The truth is that notes are not just notes—they are the best weapon in your arsenal for better learning and understanding. If you can simply add some structure and forethought into what appear to be simple notes, then the way you absorb and synthesize information will dramatically improve. Notes, though they are meant to be a recordation of what you've learned, also importantly serve as a mental blueprint for how you view the information, how it connects, and what it all means. Don't just take notes, interact with the information; chew on it and consider it fully. Do this once at the beginning and set yourself up for success.

This is just a long way of saying the obvious truth: notes are important! (A quick note on notes: writing your notes by hand has been scientifically proven to be the best method for memory and comprehension.)

The Peter Method

One powerful method of transforming information is the Peter method. The origin? Well, me! Sufficed to say, I have researched and studied the process of learning for years, and am familiar with all the existing models for notetaking out there. This method combines the best of what I've found in a system that I believe is the most thorough and helpful.

The Peter method uses four steps to take notes that lead to a deep understanding of your subject of study. The Peter method does require more work than normal notetaking, but that's part of what makes it more effective. (Sorry, there were never going to be any shortcuts in this book, just smarter approaches.)

Instead of allowing notetaking to be a brief, mostly passive exercise, the Peter method forces you to highlight the key points in your subject, and compels you to extract the salient information for yourself, in your own words. It enables you to process and elaborate upon the information you're studying in a reliable, systematic way, which makes learning and retaining the information you study infinitely easier.

The four steps are: (1) normal notetaking with as much detail as you can, (2) summarizing the information in your own words and clarifying the significance and noting questions, (3) connecting this particular piece of information to the lesson at large, and then (4) answering remaining questions and then summarizing each distinct page or section again.

The first step of the Peter method is to take notes as you ordinarily would. Copy down the information you need to know as you encounter the material, **but leave two blank lines beneath each note you take**.

These lines give you space to process and analyze the information in the second and third steps. For maximum retention, it's best to engage in these later steps immediately after you finish your class, video, or reading. So the first step is to simply carry on as you normally would in as much detail as you can.

For example, if you were researching the diet of King Henry VIII, you might write (the following is all fabricated information for the purpose of illustration), "King Henry and his court consumed up to twenty different types of meat in one sitting. Serving less was considered an insult to nobles of the time. Vegetables and wine were also served, but the focus was on the meat as it was considered a sign of wealth and status."

Step two: Once you've taken your initial notes, you move on to what really differentiates the Peter method from other forms of notetaking. It starts on the second line for each note, where you left space, and you summarize what you wrote in step one in a complete sentence. When you do this, it's important not to just repeat the initial note, even if you took your notes in complete sentences. Using your own words, converting the note to language that helps you understand the meaning of the note is essential. Ideally, you are able to abstract a deeper level of understanding. Really seek to make connections and find relationships within the information.

This isn't applicable to every piece of information, but do it anyway. Why? While it can seem redundant, the repetition itself also helps to cement the knowledge in your mind. The emphasis on repeating the knowledge in your own words, and in a fully coherent, complete sentence, requires you to process the information natively and chew on its meaning, making the information entrench itself in your mind more deeply than it would for a facile repetition.

When rephrasing the information from our example above, you might write, "Henry VIII's diet was mainly meat. In those years, rich and noble people expected a lot of different meats, and felt insulted when offered too little variety. Wine and vegetables didn't matter much."

On the second line of your notes, you can also list any questions you have about the notes you took in step one. These are points of clarification, or gaps in your knowledge, that you feel you would need to form a complete picture. Before you move on to the next step of the Peter method, consider the directions this information might lead, and what that all means. Whether you can or cannot answer it, considering the subject deeply enough to form a question will help you remember the facts.

Questions you might have about Henry VIII's diet are, "What were the health effects with such a protein-rich diet?" or "How many people were involved in getting that much meat on a daily basis, and how did they do it?" or "What did peasants eat by contrast?" or "What did other nobles from other cultures or countries consider high status?"

Use a highlighter or a different-colored pen or pencil to make this section stand out, as this is the actual information and message you've extracted from the brain dump of the first step. It's actually unlikely that you'll ever refer back to what you produced in the first step.

Step three: In the third line, the final blank line you left for yourself, state any connections you can find between the subject of that note and the broader topic you're studying. If you notice that the topic of your note has some sort of cause-and-effect relationship with the broader topic, write that here. If this new information helps understand the motivating factors or connects events or allows you to guess at people's perspective/perceptions, write those here too. Anything you can do to form lateral connections to related information should be written down here so that the links—and thus the original information—can become consistent residents of your memory banks.

The rule of thumb is to simply ask how it fits in and why it matters. Following our example, suppose the greater lesson is about Henry VIII's life and legacy. Why does information about his diet and eating habits matter?

So here you might note that the royal's diet contrasted dramatically with peasant diets, which were largely composed of fruits, vegetables, and hearty grains they farmed themselves. Perhaps this led to Henry's subjects hating and eventually executing him. You might also note that such ample, stately meals likely contributed to Henry VIII's well-known obesity. Finally, you might also see the connection that this type of opulence was a sign of how absurdly rich the nobility was at the time. Or perhaps it was just an interesting anecdote on his opulence.

Find how the information contributes to an overall narrative or story. See it as a living and breathing factor instead of a dry factoid.

Step four: The final step of the Peter method is to take a break every page (or applicable chunk) to write a summary of the information from your second and third steps. Also make sure to try to address the questions you wrote in the second step if they are still applicable.

The final step creates a fourth opportunity for you to revisit, synthesize, and transform the information you're learning on paper. If most people review information once, then you've done it four times in four different ways. To say this is helpful would be an understatement. The mental work will go a long way to making sure you truly understand and remember the facts you're learning and the implications of that information. This doesn't only help you comprehend the information but will help you apply and manipulate that information if necessary.

To finish up your notes on Henry VIII's diet, you write, "Henry VIII's court expected to consume ten types of meat with each meal. This consumption of meat was unusual at the time, as most couldn't afford much meat at all, and consumed only fruits, vegetables, and grain they could raise themselves. This may be why Henry VIII and people who ate as he did were obese. I wonder how they got so much meat, and what other health effects resulted from this diet? What effect did this type of spending have on his people's perception of him?"

As you can see, the Peter method pays notetaking the respect and attention it deserves. When we take notes, we are not just recording information, we are creating the mental blueprint for how we perceive and understand this information for all time. This is our chance at making an accurate and deeply comprehensive first impression, so we can't spoil it with normal notes. The method leads to a much deeper, much better integrated knowledge set—and that's exactly what makes information stick. If you want to remember and understand what you learn, the Peter method is the best method.

Structured Analysis

That said, the Peter method is fairly time-intensive. It's not a simple step up from normal notes. It might be too exhausting to jump right into.

Thus, a different method of notetaking that works similarly to deepen and enhance understanding, while being somewhat less taxing, is the Structured Analysis method. In this method, the student writes their notes in two columns. The left column is the Notes column, and should be about twice the width of the second column, though this ratio can be adjusted depending on your tendencies. It's a fancy name for what amounts to one additional layer of analyzing your information.

The left column contains the notes you would ordinarily take. This is where you write information about concepts, theories, and hard facts you're learning from your source. This can be done in paragraph format or in the outline format frequently taught in schools, with major and minor points differentiated from each other within the column.

The right column is the Remarks column, and this is where you'll put your analysis of what you wrote on the Notes side. This is where you answer the question, "What does this information mean?" and "What is really being said here?" and "What is the takeaway message?" Here you can also comment upon the strengths and weaknesses of theories you learn, connect the information you're studying to different things you've learned or experienced in your life, and compare and contrast the concept you're learning about with other ideas.

The idea is to line up the notes themselves and your own commentary upon those notes so that you can see the information and your own thoughts about that information at a glance. By putting your information in outlined boxes next to each other, it's easy to see what facts and concepts spawned what considerations. This can be made even clearer by using different pens to write different types of information, making reviewing the information even easier.

This method is less time consuming than the Peter method, as it requires less reiteration of the ideas you've already written (two times versus four times), but it encourages a similar level of critical thinking by leaving a space where you analyze and criticize each bit of information. Unlike simple outlines, which only contain tiered lists of facts, the Structured Analysis method reminds you to sit back and think about information and how it relates to other things you've learned or experienced in your studies and your life.

Naturally, this leads to a much deeper understanding of the information you're studying, allowing for better recall and facilitating easier employment of that information, whether it's a practical skill you're learning or something you might have to spin into a test answer later.

For example, if you're learning about Franz Kafka's book *Metamorphosis*, in which a man turns into a cockroach, you could put the main plot points of the book and the publishing data in the notes column. You might also put any potentially relevant notes about the author's life in that column. These are the bare facts you need to know about.

In the right column, you could compare and contrast his novella with other stories and novels written about metamorphoses, such as those found in Ovid. You could also speculate about philosophical or political underpinnings and meanings, and analyze the quality of the writing itself in this column. All of these—and more—will give you ample material to contemplate, not just learn by rote, the information you're studying. Much like the Peter method, this will give you a much deeper and more solid grasp of the information you're learning than you'd get by only writing down the facts you encounter.

The Doodling Effect

A final trick to transform and synthesize information better is to employ the "drawing effect," discovered by Myra Fernandes at the University of Waterloo, Canada. She and her team discovered that when people were told to make quick drawings of words on a list, they were much more likely to remember those words than they were if they only wrote those words down multiple times.

Even taking four seconds to draw a doodle was shown to be superior to looking at a picture of the words, or imagining a picture of the words internally. Drawing by hand has a major effect on memory recall; while producing a visual representation activates a different part of the brain than mere recognition, this also functions on the same principle as before—the more you chew on and manipulate information and have to reimagine it, the better you know it.

Even for more complex, abstract concepts, drawing a picture helped people recall the meanings of those words more than reading and rereading the definition. Drawing necessitates transforming that information into a new format, which requires a certain degree of understanding and ability to manipulate. The arm movements, the visual representation of the final product, and the conceptual process of deciding what to draw all seemed to play into encoding memory, and tests isolating these factors all showed lower retention than when all these parts of the process were made available to learners.

Better yet, the quality of the drawing didn't seem to matter at all. Even drawings that were almost indecipherable produced an equivalent benefit to memory—especially in the elderly, who often have trouble recalling things they write down, but remember their drawings just as easily as the young. Remember, it just has to be transformed into something that has meaning to *you*.

If you wanted to utilize the drawing effect while learning about photosynthesis, you could draw a plant, the sun, and draw lines from the sun to the plant to represent energy coming from the sun to be converted into food within the plant. Not only does this make the cycle of photosynthesis exceedingly clear and comprehensible within three seconds of looking at the drawing, it forces synthesis.

In short, taking a few seconds to doodle information to accompany your notes is a fantastic way to make sure your brain is encoding the information you're studying along even more synapses than writing alone would allow. Doodle as simple or complex as you want; the mere fact that you are attempting to create a visual *thing* is a far deeper level of information transformation that makes the difference.

I would be remiss if I didn't also mention the value of mind maps in this context. Mind maps are visual representations of notes that show relationships.

Creating a mind map is simple and very instinctual. Like the memory tree above, the first step is coming up with a central idea or theme: "tomato sauces," "repairing a car transmission," "British heraldry," "the Marvel Comics universe." Literally any broad subject you can think of is fine to put in the center.

From there, you draw lines as branches to subordinate subjects relating to your theme. For example, if you're working on tomato sauces, you could put out initial branches that refer to sauces of particular cuisines—"Italian," "Mexican," "Spanish," "Indian," "American," and so forth.

The idea is to keep on drawing branches that connect to the larger ideas. For example, under "Italian," you could list specific types of tomato sauces that originate from Italy: "marinara," "puttanesca," "Bolognese," "Arrabbiata," and so forth. Under each sauce, you can draw branches to specific ingredients, cooking tactics, good wine pairings—there really is no limit to what you can categorize with a mind map.

The organizational aspect of mind maps is another way they can reinforce memory. Relationships, connections, hierarchies, and associations are easy to represent in a mind map. And as we just discussed, visually representing relationships and associations with a certain element increases the chance that we'll remember it.

The 50-50 Rule

Finally, employing the 50-50 rule can help you transform and synthesize the information you learn. The 50-50 rule is when you spend half the time you have to study consuming information, and the other half interacting processing it—in other words, what this first pillar of self-learning has been about. This latter half is where learning actually occurs, so make sure that squandering your time on repetitive re-consumption doesn't move the needle. This entire first pillar is really an ode to the 50-50 rule.

Learning isn't something that happens when we passively encounter information; it happens when we are thinking about and communicating our knowledge with others. If you're going to err on the 50-50 rule, at least spend more time explaining and processing information than spending extra time reading or listening to someone share information with you.

If you have four hours to study a new subject in a book you have, you should be spending two hours reading that book and the next two hours processing and chewing on it. The steps in the Peter method or in the Structured Analysis method from earlier can help. What's important is to dig below the surface and understand the classic journalistic questions (*who, what, where, when, why, how*).

If you're lost for how to continue chewing and working with the information instead of mindless repetition, a tried and true method is to teach it to yourself. Of course, you're not *really* teaching it, but you're going through the mental exercise of teaching.

It's been said that if you can't communicate what you know in simple terms, you don't really know it. The longer you have to struggle to explain something, the less clear the big picture is for you. For the purposes of the 50-50 rule, you shouldn't be able to convey the information only to people who have equal knowledge and intellectual prowess to yourself. The real test of knowledge is being able to explain what you know to children in terms simple enough for them to comprehend.

You should be able to generalize enough but make distinctions that matter. This prevents you from hiding behind barely understood jargon, and will force you to gain true mastery of a topic. For instance, using the word "desalinize" if you are trying to explain the process of "desalinization" would probably indicate that you don't really know what the original term means.

While preparing to teach, it will become apparent that there are gaps in your knowledge. There will be important details or even entire processes that you won't quite grasp well enough to explain. This is an invaluable process of discovery! When this happens, that tells you exactly where you need to go back and study more thoroughly what you're learning so that you can truly master the information. Once you can communicate information simply and thoroughly in a way even children can understand, you'll know that you truly understand the subject you're studying.

Start with preparing an explanation and summary for a five-year-old. This will be simplistic and generalized, intentionally leaving out certain points that could be confusing. This might follow the formula of "X, Y, and Z, but not A." Arguably, this explanation is the most difficult because it requires the greatest overall understanding to boil things down to simplicity.

Then move to an explanation for a fifteen-year-old. This will be a bit more complex, and you will have more freedom to explain nuance and subtleties. You still have to keep things general for a teenager. This will sound more like "X, Y, and Z, but sometimes not X, sometimes A, and sometimes P." Finally, move to an explanation for a twenty-five-year-old. This is a fully formed adult who can grasp deeper and complex concepts, as well as relate them to other knowledge they already possess.

This is the easiest step because it is likely to be how you explain things to yourself. What you say here is not as important as how it contrasts to what you say to the hypothetical five-year-old.

If you go through the process of actually constructing explanations for all three levels, it will get easier, and you will find that the hard work (including the discovery that you know less than you thought) is done in the first and second levels. You can also do this whole process in reverse and start with the most complex explanation, and then keep simplifying to the point where you hit a roadblock in your understanding.

<u>Combine the New with the Familiar here</u>

The second element of our micro plan involves how we can greater understand information by looking at it through the sphere of what we already know or are familiar with. Consider how you might explain baseball to someone who only knows the game of cricket. It would be something to the effect of "it's like cricket, except A, B, and C." Obviously this is an oversimplification, but that is kind of the point—we must start somewhere, and why not with something we already know and go from there?

Imagine what learning is like for the anthropomorphized brain for a moment, if you will. It is dropped into a sea of new knowledge with no lifeboat, no map, and no visible stars in the sky. There is nothing helpful to help guide or orient what to make of this new information or concepts. It's nighttime. You have nothing to put your feet on to keep your head above water. So eventually, you give in, become overwhelmed, and drown—this is the equivalent of giving up on learning a new topic. It's important to have something to stand on or to orient ourselves with—and that is the *familiar*.

This leads us to our first point on combining the new with the familiar: analogy thinking.

Analogy Thinking

How might you explain a new business to someone who is clueless in the space? "It's like the Uber of X, except A, B, and C."

When we seek to make ourselves understand, we often default to analogies. They provide instant understanding and context, because our thoughts are able to focus on a singular concept and then slowly start to differentiate to the point of comprehension.

And of course, linking new concepts and information through analogy is another great method to cement learning into the knowledge pool. Despite our natural tendencies, analogies are underrated and overlooked as important parts of human cognition. In contrast to this presumption, some neuroscientists, such as Indiana University Professor Douglas Hofstadter, assert that analogies are the foundation of all human thought.

His reasoning is that analogies allow categories to be understood, and categories are how we discern information and concepts from each other. It's our ability to discern likenesses—a form of analogy-making—that allows us to discern similarities and thus categorize objects in different ways.

This is easy to see if you consider how we categorize animals. To an untrained eye, a dog and a cat might seem distinctly similar. They both have fur, four legs, and a tail, but their different faces, diets, and evolutionary heritage allow us to differentiate between the two of them. They are comparable animals, analogous to each other, but they are more closely analogous to their own species, and that is what allows us to place them in their respective categories of dog or cat. But all that means is that we would never use dogs to describe cats, or vice versa.

Even more complex, higher-order ideas are formed by making analogies. Consider the more abstract group of mammal. This group compares dogs to cats while counting them as similar, but also includes animals as diverse as the platypus, dolphin, and opossum. No one would look at a dolphin and believe it was similar to a housecat, but the science is very clear. Lactating, having hair or fur, and being warm-blooded are the only criteria that must be met to put creatures into the group of mammal. If they share those characteristics, they are mammals.

Grouping those criteria together allows us to form the higher-order idea of mammal, which allows us to discern which creatures fit the bill. This group of criteria that we simplify into the word mammal is what allows us to see dolphins and platypuses as analogous to each other.

Our understanding, and thus the analogies we use to describe the world, evolve as we age and are exposed to ideas in our lives and our cultures. But no matter what we learn, it must be filtered through a brain that categorizes, and thus understands, the world by forming analogies and discerning differences between objects and ideas. When we consciously discern and create analogies while learning new information, we speed up the process of integrating our new knowledge into our minds.

Now that we've covered the overall cognitive role and importance of analogy, how can we use it to effectively self-learn and understand better? As we mentioned, analogies provide instant context—a mental model for the information you are looking at—and then you are left to slowly differentiate and flesh out the details.

For instance, earlier we mentioned that new businesses are frequently described as "the Uber of X." Uber is a rideshare company that functions by calling non-taxi drivers to help transport you using their own personal cars. Thus, anything described as "the Uber of X" would be implied to involve people with their own cars, delivering or driving people or things. Okay, we've got a mental image now—a good idea of what's involved, what the purpose is, and how it functions.

Now the important bit of learning comes— how do you differentiate it from Uber itself? What nuanced factors make it simply not a clone of Uber? Well, this element, as well as what you are comparing the new business to, is up to you to articulate. When you take a new piece of information and intentionally find a way to create an analogy with it, you are (1) finding a similar model of information that requires understanding enough to compare and contrast two concepts, and (2) further understanding the two models well enough to be able to state how it differs. That's where the deeper learning synthesis occurs.

For instance, what if you wanted to create an analogy around newly learning the steps involved in creating a new piece of legislation? Abide by the two steps above. You would first find an existing, familiar piece of information that the process for new legislation reminds you of. Search your memory banks for something similar; this type of analysis of major and minor factors is helpful to your memory banks.

Next, how do they differ? This is where you can clearly demonstrate the difference between concepts, based on a deep understanding. Pick out small details and note how they appear similar but come from totally different motivations. Document what this all means for new legislation.

It's far more than a thought exercise of comparing two different concepts—it's combining old information with new and forcing them to interact toward greater comprehension and memorization.

Using Concrete Examples

Another essential technique for combining the new and the familiar is creating concrete examples to deal with abstract concepts. This is useful because abstract ideas often feel vague and are consequently hard to grasp. Human minds are wired to remember specific, concrete things we see and hear, not abstract notions about theories we contemplate. That means finding concrete examples that demonstrate abstract concepts is one of the best tools available to bring abstract notions down to Earth and make them easier to understand and remember.

As a quick example, suppose you are learning about the law of supply and demand. You will probably have some concrete examples in your textbook or lecture, but what about imposing one from your own life? Remember that time when you were trying to book a hotel in a city during peak tourism season? The prices were astronomical, and you almost had a hernia when you paid. That's because there was a huge demand, and thus, the supply was shrinking. These factors caused prices to rise, because the market demand supported higher prices where there was short supply.

Take concepts you've learned and complete this process by yourself. You may not be able to come up with concrete examples for everything you're learning, and in that case, you can use hypotheticals to literally construct examples that exemplify the point. Examples force application, and the funny thing about learning is that you'll never know what you don't know until you try to use it.

Like learning how to kick a soccer ball, we just have to find out for ourselves, and no amount of reading will ever replace firsthand experience. A concrete example is often the closest we will be able to get to much of the information and concepts we learn. Make it personal to you and you will never forget it.

Similar to analogies, the understanding required to actually construct an intelligible and illustrative example is deep. Simply going through this process will make you see the gaps in your knowledge, and also force you to revisit your entire understanding.

Suppose you are puzzled about the theory of gravity. Create an example of just how quickly you would fall to the ground if you jumped out of the second story, third story, and fourth story of a building. Visualize the concrete feeling of your stomach rushing to your throat, and you can grasp just how powerful the rate of gravity (9.8 meters per second) is. The theory of gravity is almost always told as Isaac Newton's imagining of an apple falling on his head as a very real illustration of how gravity impacts everything.

Whatever the concept, especially ones you are struggling with, strive to create your own concrete example.

For example, the mental state of *courage* is defined as "the ability to do something that frightens one." This is fairly abstract. How might we understand this better?

An obvious example would be a soldier knowingly risking his life by going to war, but fighting bravely regardless. A more accessible example would be the anxiety we feel before and during a job interview or first date, which we all try to swallow and push through to take advantage of new opportunities. This example is particularly useful, as it relates an abstract concept to a near-universal human experience the learner can remember and relate to. The more concrete it is to us, the more we feel its impact.

Even though not all examples are perfect, they add depth and meaning to our understanding while solidifying abstract concepts into ideas we can easily grasp and remember.

Self-Testing and Retrieval Practice

Retrieval practice makes us dig deep into our memory banks and work hard mentally, but at the same time, is one of the most effective ways of truly learning information. It is the third pillar of self-learning.

We typically consider learning as something we absorb—something that goes *into* our brains: the teacher or textbook spits facts, data, equations, and words out at us, and we just sit there and collect them. It's merely accumulation—a very *passive* act.

This kind of relationship with learning returns knowledge that we don't retain for very long because, even though we *get* it, we don't *do* much with it. For best results, we have to make learning an *active* operation.

That's where retrieval practice comes into play. Instead of putting more stuff *into* our brains, retrieval practice helps us take knowledge *out* of our brains and put it to use. That's what cements memory. That seemingly small change in thinking dramatically improves our chances of retaining and remembering what we learn. Everyone remembers flashcards from childhood days. The fronts of the cards had math equations, words, science terms, or images, and the backs had the "answer"— the solution, definition, explanation, or whatever response the student was expected to give.

The idea of flashcards sprouts from this concept. This approach is neither new nor very complicated: it's simply recalling information you've already learned (the back of the flashcard) when prompted by a certain image or depiction (the front).

Retrieval practice is one of the best ways to increase your memory and fact retention. But even though its core is quite simple, actually using retrieval practice isn't quite as straightforward as just passively using flashcards or scanning over notes we've taken. Rather, retrieval practice is an active skill: truly struggling, thinking, and processing to finally get to the point of recalling that information without clues— much of what we've discussed already in this book that accelerates learning.

Pooja Agarwal researched pupils taking middle school social studies over the course of a year and a half, ending in 2011. The study aimed to determine how regularly scheduled, uncounted quizzes—basically, retrieval practice exercises—benefitted the ability to learn and retain.

The class teacher didn't alter their study plan and simply instructed as normal. The students were given regular quizzes— developed by the research team—on class material with the understanding that the results would *not* count against their grades.

These quizzes only covered about a third of the material covered by the teacher, who also had to leave the room while the quiz was being taken by the students. This was so the teacher had no knowledge of what subjects the quizzes covered. During class, the teacher taught and reviewed the class as usual, without knowing which parts of the instruction were being asked on the quizzes.

The results of this study were measured during end-of-unit exams and were dramatic. Students scored one full grade level higher on the material the quizzes covered—the one-third of what the whole class covered—than the questions *not* covered on the no-stakes quizzes. The mere act of being occasionally tested, with no pressure to get all the answers right to boost their overall grades, actually helped students learn better.

Agarwal's study provided insight on what kind of questions helped the most. Questions that required the student to actually recall the information from scratch yielded more success than multiple-choice questions, in which the answer could be recognized from a list, or true/false questions. The active mental effort to remember the answer, with no verbal or visual prompt, improved the students' learning and retention.

The principal benefit of retrieval practice is that it encourages an *active* exertion of effort rather than the passive seepage of external information.

If we pull concepts *out* of our brain, it's more effective than just continually trying to put concepts *in*. The learning comes from taking what's been added to our knowledge and bringing it out at a later time. We mentioned flashcards earlier and how they're an offshoot of retrieval practice. But flashcards are not, in and of themselves, the strategy: you *can* use them and still not be conducting true retrieval practice.

Many students use flashcards inactively: they see the prompt, answer it in their heads, tell themselves they know it, flip over to see the answer, and then move on to the next one. Turning this into *practice*, however, would be taking a few seconds to actually recall the answer and, at best, say the answer out loud before flipping the card over. The difference seems slight and subtle, but it's important. Students will get more advantages from flashcards by actually retrieving and vocalizing the answer before moving on. Forcing yourself into situations like using flashcards and practice tests is what makes you remember at your best.

In real-world situations—where there's usually not an outside teacher, premade flashcards, or other assistance—how can we repurpose what we learn for retrieval practice? One good way is to expand flashcards to make them more "interactive."

The flashcards in our grade-school experiences, for the most part, were very one-note. You can adapt the methodology of flashcards for more complex, real-world applications or self-learning by taking a new approach to what's on the back of the cards.

When you're studying material for work or class, make flashcards with concepts on the front and definitions on the back. After completing this task, make another set of cards that give "instructions" on how to reprocess the concept for a creative or real-life situation. Here's an example:

- "Rewrite this concept in only one sentence."

- "Write a movie or novel plot that demonstrates this concept."

- "Use this concept to describe a real-life event."

- "Describe the *opposite* of this concept."

The possibilities are, as they say, limitless in how you can seek retrieval. Remember, your goal is to require yourself to reach into your memory, display the information, and only then put it back.

In order to make the best use of your flashcards, commit to making two sets. The first set will contain mere definitions and single concepts: one-word prompts for one-word or one-sentence answers.

The second set of flashcards will contain as much information about a single concept as possible so you will be forced to recall all of that with the prompt of a single word. This is also known as chunking information, where it's advantageous to your short-term memory (which can only hold on average seven items) to remember information as a large chunk rather than as smaller, individual components. This means that when you put more information on each flashcard, that set of information becomes one item versus five items.

When you go through your flashcards, put the cards you got wrong back into the middle or front of your stack so you see them sooner and more frequently. This helps you work through your mistakes and commit them to memory more quickly.

Using these exercises extracts more information about the concept that you produce yourself. Placing them in context of a creative narrative or expression will help you understand them when they come up in real life. Retrieval practice is simple enough with flashcards and essentially testing yourself. When you make your brain sweat a little to dig the information out of your memory and practice retrieval, you'll find that information sticks in your head extremely well. Get fancy with flashcards and prompt for information that will test the limits of your understanding and knowledge. What's important is to keep drawing the information *out*, and your memory will greatly improve.

Absorption Requires Space

Finally, we come to the fourth pillar of our micro plan: space. Absorption requires space. If it helps, think of our brains and memory banks as slow-digesting stomachs. The stomach can only digest so much food at a time. It doesn't matter if you keep force-feeding it; it will just reject or ignore the excess in the end. It doesn't matter how you massage your stomach or try to jump up and down in an attempt to jumpstart your digestive juices. The stomach's capacity is not something that can be negotiated with.

And such is the brain's capacity. This is why cramming doesn't work, and it's why anything last-minute is doomed to be a failure. To adequately learn and absorb information in a way that is actually helpful, we need to feed it to our brains at a slow and steady pace that allows it to digest; anything else will result in the excess information being rejected, vomited out, or just plain ignored. (Not to mention the great energy expenditure that our brains incur from learning.)

We can also think of our brains as elite athletes—even elite athletes have their limits where they will collapse to the ground out of exhaustion from overexertion. If we don't manage our energy by pacing our studying realistically, we won't be able to retain the information, which makes all those hours spent studying a waste.

These are all things we need to account for, and it's why more is usually not better, and why we frequently hear things like "think smarter, not harder."

One of the most successful ways to embody that maxim is *spaced repetition*.

Spaced Repetition

Spaced repetition—otherwise known as *distributed practice*—is just what it sounds like.

In order to commit more to memory and retain information better, you space out your rehearsal and exposure to it over as long of a period as possible. In other words, you learn information and skills far better if you study it for one hour each day versus twenty hours in one weekend. Similarly, research has shown that seeing something twenty times in one day is far less effective than seeing something ten times over the course of seven days. *So much for cramming.*

What does this say about how to practice? Spaced repetition is the concept that five minutes a day is far superior to learning and memory than an hour a week. When you focus on *frequency* of learning versus duration or even intensity, you will learn better. Focusing on duration usually becomes motion for motion's sake and can oftentimes become detrimental overall to your goals.

Again, think of the brain as a muscle. Muscles can't be exercised all the time and then put back to work with little to no recovery. Your brain needs time to make connections between concepts, create muscle memory, and generally become familiar with something. Sleep has been shown to be where neural connections are made, and it's not just mental. Synaptic connections are made and dendrites are stimulated in your brain.

If an athlete works out too hard in one session like you might be tempted to in studying, one of two things will happen. The athlete will either be too exhausted and the latter half of the workout will have been useless, or the athlete will become injured. Rest and recovery are necessary to the task of learning, and sometimes effort isn't what's required.

So when you focus on frequency, suddenly you have a clear structure to organize your practice with. Without a plan in place, most people will just study and practice until their eyes or fingers bleed and they collapse from exhaustion, but that's not working smart, just hard. If you follow what spaced repetition prescribes, you'll have your schedule for optimal learning set up for you.

Let's take studying for a topic you have trouble with: Spanish history. If you have trouble with this topic, that just means even more frequency should be devoted to it. A study or practice schedule focused solely on duration would be relentless from Monday to Sunday. Here's a look at what an optimized schedule focused on frequency might look like.

Monday at 10:00 a.m. Learn initial facts about Spanish history. You accumulate five pages of notes.

Monday at 8:00 p.m. Review notes about Spanish history, but don't just review passively. Make sure to try to recall the information from your own memory. Recalling is a much better way to process information than simply rereading and reviewing. This might only take twenty minutes.

Tuesday at 10:00 a.m. Try to recall the information without looking at your notes much. After you first try to actively recall as much as possible, go back through your notes to see what you missed, and make note of what you need to pay closer attention to. This will probably take only fifteen minutes.

Tuesday at 8:00 p.m. Review notes. This will take ten minutes.

Wednesday at 4:00 p.m. Try to independently recall the information again, and only look at your notes once you are done to see what else you have missed. This will take only ten minutes. Make sure not to skip any steps.

Thursday at 6:00 p.m. Review notes. This will take ten minutes.

Friday at 10:00 a.m. Active recall session. This will take ten minutes.

Looking at this schedule, note that you are only studying an additional seventy-five minutes throughout the week but that you've managed to go through the entire lesson a whopping six additional times. Not only that, you've likely committed most of it to memory because you are using active recall instead of passively reviewing your notes. Even if you take your time to be thorough and double the overall time to 150 minutes, it's still a fraction of what you would have previously spent to do far less.

It's astonishing what you can accomplish in short periods of time if you focus on frequency and don't allow yourself to drift. Scheduling relatively shorter time periods for material keeps you on your toes and prevents you from slipping into laziness if you were to schedule huge blocks of time for one task.

You're ready for a test the next Monday. Actually, you're ready for a test by Friday afternoon. Spaced repetition gives your brain time to process concepts and make its own connections and leaps because of the repetition.

Think about what happens when you have repeated exposure to a concept or skill. For the first couple exposures, you may not see anything new. As you get more familiar with it and stop going through the motions, you begin to examine it on a deeper level and think about the context surrounding it. You begin to relate it to other concepts or information, and you generally make sense of it below surface level.

There is no mindless motion: it must be active and engaged—which you can only do in short spurts. Flashcards are particularly useful for this, especially if you keep shuffling them and putting them into different orders.

It also helps to pick a different starting spot in the material for each session so you are mixing up the order and aren't just going over the same spots each time. The idea is to keep injecting freshness and different perspectives on the same material that you're seeing multiple times a day.

All of this is designed to push information from your short-term memory into your long-term memory. That's why cramming or studying at the last minute isn't an effective means of learning. Very little tends to make it into long-term memory because of the lack of repetition and deeper analysis. At that point, it becomes rote memorization instead of the concept learning we discussed earlier, which is destined to fade far more quickly.

Hopefully from this point on, instead of measuring the number of hours you spend on something, try instead to measure the number of times you can revisit it. Make it your goal to increase the frequency of reviewing, not necessarily the duration. Ideally you have both, but the literature on spaced repetition makes clear that breathing room is more important.

Spaced repetition generally has two different uses. You can use it for initial learning, but you can also use it to prevent forgetting and to ensure things stick in your brain. The above example was focused on the initial learning phase, but a sample schedule to prevent forgetting and simply keep things in mind will look a bit lighter. It will strategically touch upon information just enough to keep it in your mind, but not too much as to waste time or hit the point of diminishing returns (which is when you have already memorized it).

For example: Monday: 12 p.m., Wednesday: 12 p.m., Saturday: 12 p.m. Our brains don't necessarily want to remember more than is necessary and will dump information at the first opportunity, so spaced refreshing is far superior than one large block of time on one day.

Imagine a path in a garden that gets worn with time. The path is a memory in your brain, and it takes a certain amount of repetitions to become deep enough to stand on its own. Even a few repetitions can make a huge difference as to how clear the path becomes and how long the path will last.

If you're really pressed for time, just know that studying something twice is better than once, almost always. If you want to improve your memory and skill instantly, review something for fifteen minutes before you sleep at the end of your day. That's all it takes to get a head start on others and learn better. Just in case you are looking for a more step-by-step guideline on using spaced repetition and optimizing for frequency, here are four points.

1. Copy my study plan regarding Spanish history. Seven times a week sounds like a lot, but in reality, it ends up only being an extra one-to-two hours. This helps you keep focus and capitalizes on the way your brain prefers to absorb information. Calibrate your plan to whether you are in the initial learning phase or the "don't forget" phase.

2. Prioritize frequency—at least once a day, but ideally twice a day over the course of a week. Measure in terms of

how many times you can get through the material, repetitions, and not how long you spend on it. Again, calibrate this to whether you are in the learning phase or the "don't forget" phase.

3. Engage with the material each time and don't just go through the motions. This might require you to create different and creative ways to look at the same thing over and over. As mentioned, you can use different starting points, different flashcards, and overall different ways of reading the same material over and over. Vary the input method here.

4. Test yourself. Don't skip over things and don't just review, read, or recognize. If it feels too easy, you aren't learning optimally.

Intensity, Frequency, and Duration

We will stay on the brain as a muscle analogy for a bit longer because it informs so much of how we build our micro plan. We should build space and rest into our schedule; spaced repetition shows you why it's effective, but perhaps this next point will show you why it is absolutely necessary.

To better grasp exactly how fragile and tired our brains can be, imagine you have one hundred units of energy per day. For some of us, we only get one hundred per month. We have a finite amount of energy to spend toward learning, and this is discounting how much energy we expend in social interactions, at work, and just generally living as a human.

So how do you manage to pace yourself so you learn efficiently and prevent burnout? There are three elements you can manipulate to make sure your energy is conserved: *intensity*, *frequency*, *and duration*.

Intense, difficult learning depletes your units of energy more quickly than easier, simpler learning material. Similarly, your energy is depleted each time you study, and studying more frequently will deplete your reserves more frequently. It's also true that each minute you study takes a little more energy to keep you going, no matter how easy the material you're learning might be. Consequently, studying for a long period of time inevitably depletes a lot of your units of energy.

Intensity, frequency, and duration all have to be managed. You can allot 33 units of energy to each, but this is going to wear you down fast.

Intensity can be determined by the difficulty of your topic, but more often than not, it's just about how much effort you have to expend in a given hour. Reading is not so intense, while a practice test is very intense. You can also use this to measure your expectations—if you want to just get by, it will not be so intense, but if you want perfection, expect to expend more effort. Lowering your expectations lowers your stress level and makes the study session less draining.

Frequency of study is the second factor you need to consider when setting expectations for your progress. Each time you study will drain your energy a little bit, and the more difficult the topic is, the more quickly it will drain your reserves each time. If you aim to study during every bit of downtime you have, it ends up being too much of a good thing, because your brain might not get the downtime it needs to integrate your new knowledge, and of course, the space it needs. Our brains need rest to function! If you feel worn out and unable to think at any point, you might be studying too frequently and should slow down a bit.

Duration of study is the last factor that must be controlled to prevent intellectual burnout. The longer each study session lasts, the more likely your studying is to be inefficient by the end. During sessions that are truly too long, the mind will shut off by the middle or end of the session, making it almost impossible to understand or integrate new information any longer. Remember, humans have limited stores of energy. We can't expect to spend more energy than we have in a single session. Shorter, more frequent sessions often allow the mind to rest and recuperate for maximum intellectual progress. Plan accordingly.

To abide by the commandment of absorption requiring space, when you are learning, you can only focus on two of the three factors maximum at one time. There are six permutations, but to focus on all three will just leave you drained and your brain in a mode where it won't absorb anything at all.

So for instance, if you focus on only intensity and frequency, intense study sessions every day will allow your mind and body to rest and properly synthesize. To take it to the next level of intensity and frequency, five minutes several times per day quizzing yourself on facts. You almost ignore duration, but since these mini-sessions are so intense and frequent, you are learning more in the end.

If you want to crank up the duration of your sessions, it either needs to be less intense or less frequent—two hours every three days, for instance. Leave your brain the room it needs, and the results you want will follow.

You might be dedicated, but your brain can't match it. It's essential to remember this when managing your own studying, and to take it into account when scheduling your own sessions.

Consider Jerry, who likes studying philosophy. He's been reading original sources for a few years, and isn't intimidated by most of the great thinkers in history. Next on his list of thinkers to study is Hegel. Now, Hegel is a bit special. Historically, he's been accused of being deliberately confusing. That is to say, his concepts, once you know what they are, aren't terribly complicated, but his manner of writing goes around in circles and often communicates those insights in the most complicated way imaginable.

This makes his ideas difficult to understand, which means that any study of his work is going to be intense—it will drain the energy of the student quickly, as real brainpower is required to figure out what the man was saying in his walls of verbiage.

But Jerry is determined. He sets aside a few hours every night, sits down, and puts the book in front of him. "I'll study a whole chapter every night," he asserts, "and I should finish in no time."

He reads and reads and reads. At first, he stops frequently to make notes. He leaves space to add his thoughts, and occasionally makes notes about the implications of what he's reading and other ideas and questions the text brings to mind. It's the beginning of his session, and he's doing fine. He's even enjoying the process, because that's who Jerry is.

But after half an hour, he notices his attention drifting. He finds himself getting distracted. He wonders what he'll make for dinner, what his best friend is doing, and whether he needs to do laundry anytime soon. Each time his mind wanders, he determines to study harder, but the interruptions are becoming more and more frequent.

He squints at the page in determination, his frustration building as he pushes himself. As he continues to study, each page takes longer than the last to complete. Within twenty more minutes, he finds the words slipping by him as he reads. What did Hegel just say? Why did he not understand it well enough to write himself notes on his reading? The answer is simple: he pushed himself to the point of exhaustion, and no one can learn in that state. The intensity of his studying was simply too high for the long-duration, high-frequency study schedule he wanted to follow.

Over time, you will be able to find your *Goldilocks Zone* where your studying isn't too intense, too frequent, or too long in any single session. Once you do, you'll be able to balance the three factors to maximize the learning you're capable of doing while preventing exhaustion and burnout.

Remember, the more complex your material is, the more time you will need to devote to studying that subject. The longer you study in a single session, the more time you will need between sessions to ensure complete processing and absorption of what you're studying. You can combine intensity, duration, or frequency, but never all three. Don't burn yourself out, or learning the new information or acquiring the new skills you seek will take longer and be more frustrating than necessary. Remember, study smarter, not harder, if you want to attain your goals.

Takeaways:

- In the first chapter, we introduced the notion that there are no true requirements for effective self-learning. This eliminates most of the myths surrounding learning and how the brain functions, but that's a good thing. The only thing that is truly required is a plan to ensure that you are moving forward and achieving your learning goals.
- This chapter introduces the four elements of the *micro* plan—in other words, what we should actually be doing beyond reading, listening, and watching. The way that we interact with information is learning itself, and we must be intentional with our methods.
- The first element of our micro plan is transforming information into something personal to us. This is another extremely active way to interact with information. Most people passively absorb information as if through

osmosis, but that is inefficient at best. When we simply take information or concepts and put it into our own words, we process it differently, even if only through repetition. We can do this through taking great notes with the four-step Peter method (take normal notes, summarize the notes and ask questions, connect the information to the topic at large, and then re-summarize to take context into account) or the Structured Analysis method of taking notes. Doodling and drawing also has a marked effect on better understanding, as well as being heavily related to how mind maps function. In the end, we come upon a guiding principle: when we are learning, we should aim to spend no more than fifty percent of our time consuming, and rather devote more time to processing and analyzing the new information.

- The second element of the micro plan is about combining new information and concepts with what we are already familiar with. This step may not come naturally, but thinking in analogies and creating concrete examples with the information you've gained will cement your comprehension. They both require a deeper conceptual understanding of what you've learned, and in addition, they may uncover more thorough levels of knowledge. When you are able to use analogies and examples with new information, it is a sign of mastery.

- The third element is self-testing and practicing drawing information out of your brain instead of trying to stuff information into it. This may be counterintuitive, but the more we can engage in mini tests, the better we memorize and learn. This is known as retrieval practice, as you are retrieving information. Though this is mostly done through the context of flashcards, the overarching lesson is that we must be active in our efforts. The bigger the struggle, the deeper the learning and memorization. When you force yourself to learn, well, you will learn. There is no real shortcut.
- The fourth element of the micro plan is to be stingy with your mental and

physical energy. The brain is like a muscle in that it can't work all day and all night and still function well. One of the key techniques that help guard against this is spaced repetition, which implores you to focus on frequency rather than duration of learning. This has been proven to be more effective than most other conventional study schedules. In fact, there are three factors that we should be mindful of when we try to give ourselves the space for absorption to occur: intensity, frequency, and duration. We can only focus on, at best, two at a time, so make sure you are not setting yourself up for failure and burnout.

Chapter 3. Tactics for Learning

Clarice's company is hosting a charity auction to raise funds for their organization. Clarice's responsibility is to search through the organization's records to find likely donors based on their past interactions with the organization, collect those names on a list with the potential donors' contact information, and address envelopes to each of the people who meet enough criteria to be invited to the event.

This task is simple enough, but Clarice was told to add this duty to the workload she already completes in the office, a workload that—though manageable—rarely left her with extra time during the day.

For two weeks, she kept showing up to work and completing her ordinary tasks. But honestly, she had a short attention span and couldn't focus for more than ten minutes at a time before checking her phone. Her heart was in it, but her effort was lacking. This compounded because as stress stymied her mind, she took more breaks to try to regain her composure and her hope, but nothing was good enough.

Distracted by her other tasks, she waited too long to tackle the new project. She was never going to finish the list before the mailings had to be shipped. Ultimately, she confessed her failure to her boss and needed to be helped by others in the office to complete her task in a timely manner. Because Clarice couldn't figure out how to manage her attention span and focus effectively, she failed to complete her task and held her whole team back.

Managing Your Attention Span

Despite the fact that classes in school can last for an hour or more, humans are not good at paying attention to one thing for an extended period of time. At the biological level, we are programmed to pay attention to multiple things for short periods of time, instead of focusing on one object. Of course, we can attribute this to our propensity for staying alive by fleeing at the first sign of danger. This biologically leads to short attention spans, and we must learn to account for this in our learning endeavors.

Multiple studies have investigated exactly how long our attention spans are; in one early study, scientists noticed that the quality of the notes students took during a lecture declined in quality as the lecture went on. This led them to posit that human attention spans were ten-to-fifteen minutes long and that we have difficulty paying attention to information after that much time passes.

A different study utilized trained observers to watch students for lapses in attention during a lecture. They noticed peak inattention in three spots: during the initial settling-in period, ten-to-eighteen minutes into the lecture, and toward the end of the lecture. Indeed, by the final ten minutes, they noticed students failing to pay attention as often as every three-to-four minutes. Their conclusion was that declines in attentiveness occur over time, and there is a certain acclimatization period at the beginning, during which we are particularly susceptible to losing focus.

A third study provided students with clickers to press when they found themselves being inattentive during class. This time, the researchers had students sit in on three different types of classes. Some students sat in on a lecture course, others needed to pay attention to a demonstration, and others were in a question-and-answer session. Each student, regardless of the type of class they attended, was provided a clicker with three different buttons. One was pressed to record a lapse in attention of a minute or less, one was pressed to indicate lapses of two-to-four minutes, and the other was meant to indicate lapses of attention of five minutes or more. This data was then mapped onto the lecture or demonstration people attended to observe how a lesson's style impacted student attentiveness.

They discovered that the majority of lapses were less than a minute long, suggesting that students were much more likely to momentary fade out than to be distracted for an extended period of time. Most of the time, the students were paying attention.

They also discovered that lapses in attention were sooner than the ten-minute estimate previous studies would lead people to expect. Inattention spiked in the students thirty seconds after arriving to class, during the "settling in" period, at 4.5 to 5.5 minutes into class, at seven-to-nine minutes into class, and at nine-to-ten minutes in. Attention of the class as a whole continued to wax and wane with this pattern as the class continued, though there were more lapses in attention toward the end of class, when spikes of inattention could be observed every two minutes.

Perhaps the most interesting finding of this study is that the scientists noted much fewer lapses in attention in the demonstration and question-based teaching styles. When students were more active participants in their classroom experience rather than passive listeners, they stayed engaged more often and for longer periods of time. Taking one of these classes before a lecture course even made that lecture course easier, and students in that position were found to pay attention for longer periods and lapse less frequently. It seems that active learning engages human attention and refreshes it for subsequent, more passive learning sessions.

In short, humans do indeed have almost laughably short attention spans. No matter how flawed the data or study might be, there is a clear consensus of it being only a matter of minutes. But this is not a fate we are resigned to; we aren't limited to a set short attention span all the time. By using active and engaging learning methods, we can turn attention lapses into minuscule blips and radically improve our learning output.

Consider this an extension of the previous chapter's recommendation that you take your energy levels into account. As it turns out, our capacity for learning is almost never limited by the time we have; it is more often limited by the energy and attention we have.

Pomodoro and Friends

A practice that can help you push past distractions and train yourself into a hyper-focused state is the *Pomodoro Technique*. Even better, this method reminds you to take occasional breaks to keep you alert and maximize your productivity.

The Pomodoro Technique was invented in the 1990s by a developer, author, and entrepreneur named Francesco Cirillo. He discovered that if he broke his work schedule down into short sections he timed with his tomato-shaped timer, his ability to focus on his work was improved. Over time, he even found that his attention span lengthened and his ability to concentrate on single projects over a longer period of time improved.

More than that, the timed and scheduled system of working reminded him to take regular breaks, which increased his motivation to work and improved his ability to solve problems creatively. He named his new technique *pomodoro*, after the timer that facilitated the whole process.

If you also want to enhance your productivity, increase your attention, and improve your concentration while taking time to relax and recuperate, the Pomodoro Technique could be perfect for you. Here's how you do it:

First, choose a task to complete. If you have several tasks to complete, or your task is very long and complex, you will need to break your work into smaller tasks that can be completed within twenty-five minutes. Of course, for us, this will always be in the context of learning, whether consuming or analyzing and processing information.

For example, if you want to read a book, you can divide it into twenty-five-minute sections based on your reading speed, perhaps slightly more than you think you can fit in. You can always keep working after the timer goes off, but if you run out of things to do during a pomodoro, you won't be able to complete the unit uninterrupted. You don't want that!

Second, set your timer to twenty-five minutes. This will define the length of time you'll be working without any breaks or interruptions.

Cirillo believes that a physical timer you can twist to twenty-five minutes is the best method to use, as this allows you to physically rev yourself up for work by ritualistically moving the timer with your hands. It's worth investing in a timer to add this element to your sessions.

Third, work, study, or learn until the timer rings. Once it rings, you can put a checkmark or a sticker onto a piece of paper so that you know how many pomodoros you've managed to complete in a single day. This lets you track your progress and really see how much time you've dedicated to your project.

You can get a whiteboard to put up in your work and study area, or you can tape a piece of paper to the wall to track your progress. The whole point is to remain aware of what you're doing and to take pride in the number of pomodoros you manage to complete. Uninterrupted sessions are something to be proud of!

Fourth, take a short break. Five minutes is a good period of time for a break, but it doesn't have to be exact. The whole point is to rest, stretch, and get yourself into good shape for another pomodoro. Keep it short!

When you're done with a pomodoro, you can watch a YouTube video, go for a walk, or take a break to get a cup of water, tea, or coffee. Getting up, moving around, and relaxing your mind is the order of the day. But don't get too far off track, and don't you dare engage in anything that will take longer than five minutes.

Fifth, every four pomodoros, take a longer break. This break can last between fifteen and twenty-five minutes, but should really be as long as you need to rest, recuperate, and feel fresh and ready to start another pomodoro. This is your chance to really unwind for a bit; stretch your mental muscles, but know that you are probably in for another set of four pomodoros.

During your longer breaks, you can read about something else, spend time on your favorite social media sites, or even take a power nap. With a longer break, you have even more options for your own enjoyment. And after four pomodoros, you can do it guilt-free, because you've already done a good amount of studying or learning that day.

An essential aspect of this productivity method is that a pomodoro is an inviolable, indivisible period of work. You can't start your timer, get distracted, and count the time you weren't working as a valid pomodoro. If you're interrupted or discover yourself spacing out, you have to stop your pomodoro and restart it when you're ready to begin again. The whole point of the method is to train yourself to be productive and to focus for twenty-five whole minutes; if you fail, you start again until your brain gets used to the rhythm. Sooner or later, you will become accustomed to the pace, and it'll be a lot easier to focus and pound out work for the whole pomodoro.

Interruptions from other people are harder to control, but Cirillo teaches a method to overcome that possibility, too. His advice is to follow the "inform, negotiate, call back" method to handle untimely interruptions. Using it involves a four-step process.

First, inform the person who approaches you that you're busy right now and can't interrupt your work for them at the moment.

Second, negotiate when you can get back to them so that they know you aren't going to ignore their needs in favor of work.

Third, schedule a follow-up. Setting a specific time to get back to them will reassure them and make them more likely to leave you to your pomodoro.

Fourth and finally, call them back when your pomodoro is complete. Because you rescheduled their interruption, it becomes your responsibility to get back to them and engage with their needs.

This method doesn't have to be complicated. Simply saying, "I can't interrupt my work right now. Can I call you back in ten minutes (or however long is left in your pomodoro)?" fulfills three of four steps. All you have to do after that is call them when your timer goes off. The ring to remind you to stop working then becomes a reminder to get in touch with the other person! After one or two times doing this, your coworkers, family, or friends will understand what you're doing and trust you to get back to them reliably, allowing you to continue your pomodoros uninterrupted. Almost nothing (within reason) is ever so urgent that it can't wait twenty-five minutes, or even two hours. The only thing that is urgent is the way you get distracted.

Remember, despite the strict need to continue pomodoros for the entire twenty-five minutes, they're not a prison sentence. You are more than able to continue work past the twenty-five-minute timer as long as you remember to take a break once the chunk of work you chose to do is finished. Breaks also increase productivity by keeping you refreshed and ready for work at all hours of the day. Work, then rest.

After you've trained on the Pomodoro Technique for a while, it's possible to increase your attention span and improve your concentration even further by doubling the timespan into the *50-10 rule*. This encourages you to set your study and productivity timer to fifty instead of twenty-five minutes, and lets you take a break twice as long once you finish. The benefit of this is that you're resting and recuperating and pursuing other interests just as much, but your ability to focus and be productive should be even more finely honed and well-disciplined. Being able to do more for longer, without needing to take a break or being distracted by interruptions, is always a good thing. You'll probably have to work up to this.

When the 50-10 rule becomes easy and manageable, you can push yourself one step further into the *60-60-30 method*.

The 60-60-30 method involves working for sixty minutes twice, and then resting for thirty minutes. More specifically, it suggests using two iterations of the 50-10 method back to back, and then following those two sessions with resting for thirty minutes. Setting a timer when you work and rest allows you to avoid looking at the clock, and at this point, working or studying for fifty minutes straight should feel fairly natural. This method just amps up the process further while reminding you to stay refreshed and rested while you're getting stuff done.

Overall, it should be clear why these methods of focusing are successful at battling your short attention span. To effectively learn, you must first be able to pay attention.

Change Locations

Changing location sounds like it doesn't have anything to do with memory and learning, so how does it tie into the rest of this chapter?

Our memories are not just triggered when we want to recall them consciously. They are sometimes unconsciously triggered because they are associated with everything that was present when we made that memory. That's why smells or songs can instantly transport us to another time and place. The smell or song was present when the memory was formed, and thus a single memory can have multiple triggers, conscious or not.

A significant portion of our cognition and thinking occurs unconsciously, and it would be foolish of us to not integrate this into our learning practices. Why not use our primitive brains to help us remember facts and concepts, instead of just making us hungry and thirsty?

This tactic is about the phenomenon that studying the same material in different locations and environments helps memory retention. This is known as *context-dependent memory*, and it is based on findings that learning is not very exclusive when it occurs. In fact it is very inclusive.

A study by Robert Bjork found that information is remembered and encoded into our memory *holistically*. This means that if you study Spain in an aquarium, your memory will associate the two subconsciously. Your memory will also associate what you wore that day, what you ate, the smells in the aquarium, and what stood out visually in your environment. As far as your memory is concerned, they'll all be lumped together with the specific information you are trying to remember or learn. Information is information to the brain, whether it comes from a textbook or our senses or the environment.

This means two things.

First, that it is possible to evoke the memory of Spain just by being exposed to the same smells and visual stimuli. If they are part of your overall memory of the information, then they will act to remind you of the rest of it. In other words, if you studied Spain in an aquarium and see a picture of an aquarium, it's entirely possible that it will remind you of the information you learned about Spain. Lots of unconscious associations have the ability to trigger information that you consciously want.

Second, if you change locations frequently while learning and processing the same information, you are strengthening your memory because it will be associated with multiple locations, smells, and general stimuli to make you remember it. Researchers deemed this *increased neural scaffolding*. Simply put, for one piece of information about Spain, you can have ten different environmental factors that can help you recall it from memory. The more stimuli that triggers that memory or information, the more deeply it is encoded in your memory like a growing web.

What does this mean for you? You should change locations as frequently as possible while learning the same information. If you can't change your scenery completely, change what's on your desk, the music you are listening to—anything that impacts any of your five senses. The more change of stimuli, the more roots the information will take to your brain.

Scientists have found other links between what memories can be associated with. Ruth Propper of Montclair State University found that even muscle contractions, namely a clenched right fist, could be subconsciously associated with information and memory if done simultaneously. One group of participants clenched a ball with their right fists while performing a memory task, while other groups either had no ball at all or clenched their left fists.

The first group routinely performed the best. Why does this work? It could be similar to why changing locations increases memory retention, because the more stimuli, the more cues for the information. Just think of these phenomena as creating more roads to the information you want in your brain. Each time you switch locations or associate the information with something else, you build more roads for easier access and deeper encoding.

For instance, if you are studying and learning from 9 a.m. to 3 p.m., that's six hours. You can plan to switch locations every two hours. This helps with your contextual encoding and retrieval. To take it to the next level, you can add in different temperatures, sounds, smells, and sights for each location—each of the five senses can help you make and recall memories.

To take full advantage of everything these scientific studies have demonstrated, expose yourself to different situations, locations, and contexts while studying. Split your study session into different locations and stimuli every hour or two. Switch locations. Mix things up and make it a habit to move around. Remember, this is what gives your information more roots to take hold in your brain and to be recalled with.

Though we typically eschew absorbing information passively, it actually works to our favor in this case—for *indirect* information. You don't even need to be paying specific attention to the environmental factors to gain the benefits of being there.

Construct Vivid Imagery

Constructing vivid imagery—off the top of your head, can you guess why this helps your learning? Here is a simple example. When you think about your past year, what do you remember, boring things or exciting things? Undoubtedly you remember the exciting things because they made an impact on you. That is something we can replicate in our everyday quest for learning and better memory.

A large body of research indicates that visual cues help us better retrieve and remember information. The research on visual learning make sense when you consider that our brain is mainly an image processor, not a word processor. In fact, the part of the brain used to process words is quite small in comparison to the part that processes visual images—roughly thirty percent of the brain is devoted to visual imagery alone.

Words are abstract and rather difficult for the brain to retain, whereas visuals are concrete and, as such, more easily remembered.

To illustrate, think about having to learn a set of new vocabulary words each week. Now, think back to the first kiss you had or your high school prom date. Most probably, you had to put forth great effort to remember the vocabulary words. In contrast, when you were actually having your first kiss or your prom date, I bet you weren't trying to commit them to memory. Yet, you can quickly and effortlessly visualize these experiences (now, even years later). You can thank your brain's amazing visual processor for your ability to easily remember life experiences. Your brain memorized these events for you automatically and without you even realizing what it was doing.

There are countless studies that have confirmed the power of visual imagery in learning. For instance, one study asked students to remember many groups of three words each, such as dog, bike, and street. Students who tried to remember the words by repeating them over and over again did poorly on recall. In comparison, students who made the effort to make visual associations with the three words, such as imagining a dog riding a bike down the street, had significantly better recall.

The effective use of visuals can decrease learning time, improve comprehension, enhance retrieval, and increase retention. If our brain is wired for vision, and we typically remember vivid, bright, and intense information, then we should combine the two. Mentally constructing vivid imagery helps us remember.

For instance, take a list of eight objects you want to memorize: rabbit, coffee, blanket, hair, cactus, running, mountain, and tea.

This would seem to be incredibly difficult to memorize because everything is unrelated. However, you can give yourself a better chance by creating a vivid and striking mental image for each item. It doesn't have to be a literal representation of the word, or even related to it.

For instance, what images can you create for rabbit? You could use a mental image of a normal, cute rabbit, but that's not likely to be distinctive in your memory. You could conjure up an image of what the word rabbit makes you think of, a symbol, what the word sounds like to you, or how the word is written. The more outrageous and unusual, the better for you to memorize, because we tend to easily forget normal things.

When you put this same amount of thought into the eight items of that list, you will be able to memorize them more effectively. It's not just taking advantage of how your brain works; it's the attention and time to choosing an appropriate mental image. Recall how we discussed the power of doodling, as it related to both activating our visual processing neurons as well as simply putting more time and effort into the exercise of drawing something. It's not about the doodle or imagery itself, it's about the attention you pay and the time you spend.

You can use this with lists, information, and even difficult-to-grasp concepts. When you can get into the habit of not taking information at face value and constructing vivid imagery to make it stand out in your mind, you'll remember things far better. Just say no to learning by osmosis!

Constructing vivid imagery can actually take another form. A quick question—what do you remember better, a boring movie or an exciting movie? Of course, you remember the exciting movie better because of the impact it made on you, and in a word, it was memorable.

So let's start with an illustration of this for you to immediately feel the difference a vivid *story* can make.

First things first, try to memorize the same words in this order: rabbit, coffee, blanket, hair, cactus, running, mountain, tea.

Now, take a sheet of paper and write down the words you remember in the exact order they were listed. See how many you can remember.

Most people can remember between three to four words. If you got more than that, that's great. As you can see, relying on just your natural memory isn't the best idea. If you can get fifty percent of the items on the list, that's considered good. But that's not a good baseline for learning!

Now we come to the point of this technique, which is to create a story that involves all those items. When you can create meaningful connections between items instead of trying to memorize dry facts, you stand a better chance. A story ends up being one large piece of information rather than eight distinct pieces; this is similar to what happens when you attempt to connect old and new information from earlier in this book.

By creating a story for those words, you'll be able to memorize all of them in the correct order far more easily. What kind of story might you construct with the list we have? As with the previous method, the more unusual and outrageous, the better and more memorable it will be. Vivid things tend to stick, so you need to engage and find a way to make things stand out to you.

As a reminder: rabbit, coffee, blanket, hair, cactus, running, mountain, tea.

It could start with a rabbit who went to jail for selling drugs hidden with coffee. He has now tried to attack his cellmates in jail by making weapons with his blanket and hair tied together. However, one day, he found a cactus while running outside in the prison yard. By trading this cactus for three kilograms of tea, he was able to escape to the mountains above the jail and was never seen again.

One item is a brain trigger that helps you remember the next item. It's similar to hearing a song and each verse brings you to remember the next verse and you can remember all the words to a song.

The main principles of this technique are to make each item distinctive (imagination) and link it to the next one (association). The crazier you can make the story, the better. The more distinctive, the more it will stick in your mind. When you make up your story, visualize it in your head with as much color and movement as possible. Practice the story two or three times. Then, test yourself to see how many you can remember. Like I've said before, these techniques to improve memory are so effective because they're a reflection of how memory works.

The main idea is to create meaning from meaningless and unrelated facts or information, which of course, makes it easier to remember.

The Question Master

We saved an important tactic for last—how to become a *question master*.

The importance of being a question master cannot be overstated; it's not about being pedantic or provocative. We've said multiple times that you can't expect information to teach you or to make itself understood. This responsibility will always fall upon you in the end. If you're not getting or understanding something from a lecture, book, or video, the answer surely cannot be to keep reading the same passage over and over.

You must make an effort to investigate and pull understanding out yourself. It just makes you think of psychology experiments where rats continue to shock themselves by pressing a lever. No progress is being made, so obviously the approach needs to change. It's a clear example of working smarter, not harder; no one can deny that the rat works hard, but with questionable results.

Let's consider two people who read the same book on Spanish history. Jimbo will read along and review the information. He will take notes and can pass a test quite easily on the subject. His answers read like bullet points for a recipe for cornbread. He receives a B+. Kudos for Jimbo.

Kunal, on the other hand, reads the same book, but he only does this once or twice, and instead spends the rest of his time trying to gain a deeper understanding of the whys and motivations of Spanish conquistadors and kings. He attains an A+ on the same test, a better mark because he displayed a deeper insight that Jimbo could ever possess. His answers are more like essays, and even though he forgot a couple minute details, he made insightful leaps of reasoning and judgment because of his deeper understanding.

He achieved this level of mastery by asking probing questions and using them to get behind facts and information. He processed the information and chewed on it with his questions. He finds that he doesn't even need to know all the facts if he asks the right questions, because he can predict what the conquistadors would probably have done. Kudos for Kunal.

In learning, it is said that answers are far less important than questions people ask. Indeed, we've also heard this advice in relation to job interviews, where you should always have "intelligent questions" to display that you understand the interviewing company on a deeper level.

Rote memorization of information is sometimes the goal, but if we ever want to understand and comprehend more deeply, questions are the first place to start. Questions will take a flat piece of information and turn it into a living, three-dimensional piece of knowledge that interacts with the world at large. That is the reality of any fact or piece of information; it has a story we are usually overlooking in the interest of speed or efficiency. To ask a question is to see a subject, identify what you don't know, and also be open to the fact that your entire understanding could be wrong. Meaningful learning only occurs when you understand what surrounds information, such as the background and context.

Put another way, good questions end up allowing us to *triangulate* understanding. Take a textbook, for example. It is necessarily broad and cannot hope to cover all the subtleties involved. If we fully accept what we read, then we are set on a singular path. If we ask questions, we are able to see that the path itself contains twists and turns and may not even be accurate. Different lines of inquiry are generated, and it is understood that there are multiple paths, each with their own perspective. Questions allow us to both clarify misunderstandings and reinforce what we already know. In the end, we come to an understanding of the same textbook that is nuanced and more accurate.

Luckily for us, teachers have known this for literally thousands of years. The most helpful framework for generating insightful questions comes from no other than Socrates himself, the ancient Greek philosopher perhaps best known for being Plato's teacher, as well as being executed by the state for "corrupting the minds of the youth." His method of teaching was largely in the form of dialogues and questions, appropriately called the *Socratic Method*.

When you boil it down, the Socratic Method is when you ask questions upon questions in an effort to dissect an assertion or statement for greater understanding. The person asking the questions might seem like they are on the offensive, but they are asking questions to enrich both parties and discover the underlying assumptions and motivations of the assertion or statement. It is from this process that we have a framework for effective questioning.

Imagine that you make a proclamation, and the only response you get is a smug, "Oh, is that so? What about X and Y?" Unfortunately, the know-it-all questioner is on the right path.

American law schools are notorious for using the Socratic Method. A professor will ask a student a question, and then the student will have to defend their statement against a professor's questioning regarding the merits of a case or law. It's not adversarial by nature, but it does force someone to explain their reasoning and logic—and of course, gaps in knowledge and logical flaws will probably surface. This process serves the goal of deeper understanding and insight. It may cause defensiveness, though it is not offensive in itself.

So what exactly is the Socratic Method beyond asking a series of tough questions that make people uncomfortable? When you do it to yourself, you are forcing understanding. You are putting yourself through an incredible stress test that will make you question yourself and your logic. It will force you to discard your assumptions and see what you might be missing. If you are mercilessly questioned and picked apart with Socratic questioning, what remains afterward will be deeply comprehended and validated. If there is an error in your thinking or a gap in your understanding, it will be found, corrected, and proofed with a rebuttal. That's deep learning.

As a brief example, imagine that you are telling someone that the sky is blue.

This seems like an unquestionable statement that is an easy truth. Obviously, the sky is blue. You've known that since you were a child. You go outside and witness it each day. You've told someone that their eyes were as blue as the sky. But remember, our goal with questions is to better acquire knowledge as to the sky's blueness. So imagine someone asks *why* you know it is blue.

There are many ways to answer that question, but you decide to say that you know the sky is blue because it reflects the ocean, and that the ocean is blue, even though this is erroneous. The questioner asks how you know it is a reflection of the ocean.

How would you answer this?

This brief line of Socratic questioning just revealed that you have no idea why or how the sky reflects (or doesn't) the blue of the planet's oceans. You just attempted to explain an underlying assumption, and you were mildly surprised to discover that you had no idea.

That, in a nutshell, is the importance of the Socratic Method. A series of innocent and simple questions directed at yourself, honestly and earnestly answered, can unravel what you thought you knew and lead you to understand exactly what you don't know. This is often just as important as knowing what you do know because it uncovers your blind spots and weaknesses.

Recall that it was used by teachers as as teaching tool, so it is designed to impart deeper understanding and clarify ambiguities.

There are six types of Socratic questions as delineated by R.W. Paul. After just briefly glancing at this list, you might understand how these questions can improve your learning and lead you to fill in the gaps in your knowledge.

The six types of questions are:

1. Clarification questions—why exactly does it matter?
2. Probing assumptions—what hidden assumptions might exist?
3. Probing rationale, reasons, evidence—what proven evidence exists?
4. Questioning viewpoints and perspectives—what other perspectives exist?
5. Probing implications and consequences—what does this mean, what is the significance, and how does it connect to other information?

6. Questions about the question—why is this question important?

Clarification questions: What is the real meaning of what is being said? Is there an underlying hidden motivation or significance to this piece of information? What do they hope to achieve with it? Suppose we have the same assertion from above, where the sky is blue. Here are some sample questions from each category you could plausibly ask to gain clarity and challenge their thoughts.

- What does it matter to you if the sky is blue?
- What is the significance to you?
- What is the main issue here?
- What exactly do you mean by that?
- What does that have to do with the rest of the discussion?
- Why would you say that?

Probing assumptions: What assumptions are the assertions based on and are actually supported by evidence? What is opinion and belief, and what is evidence-based fact or proven in some other way? Unless you are reading a scientific paper, there are always inherent assumptions that may or may not be accurate.

- Is your blue my blue?
- Why do you think the sky is blue?
- How can you prove or verify that?
- Where is this coming from exactly?
- So what leads you to believe the sky is blue?
- How can you prove that the sky is blue?

Probing rationale, reasons, and evidence: How do you know the evidence is trustworthy and valid? What are the conclusions drawn, and what rationale, reasons, and evidence are specifically used in such a way? What might be missing or glazed over?

- What's the evidence for the sky's color, and why is it convincing?
- How exactly does the ocean's reflection color the sky?
- What is an example of that?
- Why do you think that is true?

- What if the information was incorrect or flawed?
- Can you tell me the reasoning?

Questioning viewpoints and perspectives: People will almost always present an assertion or argument from a specific bias, so play the devil's advocate and remain skeptical about what they have come up with. Ask why opposing viewpoints and perspectives aren't preferred and why they don't work.

- How else could your evidence be interpreted, an alternative view?
- Why is that research the best in proving that the sky is blue?
- Couldn't the same be said about proving the sky is red? Why or why not?
- What are the potential flaws in this argument?
- What is the counterargument?
- Why doesn't the sky color the ocean instead of the other way around?

Probing implications and consequences: What are the conclusions and why? What else could it mean, and why was this particular conclusion drawn? What will happen as a consequence, and why?

- If the sky is blue, what does that mean about reflections?
- Who is affected by the sky's color?
- What does this information mean, and what are the consequences?
- What does this finding imply? What else does it determine?
- How does it connect to the broader topic or narrative?
- If the sky is blue, what does that mean about the ocean?
- What else could your evidence and research prove about the planet?

Questions about the question: This is less effective when you are directing this question to yourself. Directed towards someone else, you are forcing people to ponder why you asked the question or why you went down that line of questioning, and realize that you had something you wanted to evoke. What did you mean when you said that, and why did you ask about X rather than Y?

- So why do you think I asked you about your belief in the sky's color?
- What do you think I wanted to do when I asked you about this?
- How do you think this knowledge might help you in other topics?
- How does this apply to everyday life and what we were discussing earlier?

At first, it sounds like a broken record, but there is a method to the madness. Each question may seem similar, but if answered correctly and adequately, they go in different directions. In the example of the blue sky, there are over twenty separate questions—twenty separate answers and probes into someone's simple assertion that the sky is blue. You can almost imagine how someone might discover that they know next to nothing and are only able to regurgitate a limited set of facts without context or understanding.

You can apply the Socratic Method to ensure that you are understanding what you think you are understanding. You can think of it as a systematic process of examining and just double-checking yourself. The end result will always be a win, as you either confirm your mastery or figure out exactly what is missing from your mastery.

Suppose you hear from a friend that the Spanish Inquisition was a fairly humane process of light interrogation, with only very humane maimings and lashings (various sources put the death toll at, on average, around one hundred thousand people). In this instance, you can use the Socratic questions to correct a mistake. The six question types, as a reminder:

1. Clarification questions—why does it matter?
2. Probing assumptions—what hidden assumptions might exist?
3. Probing rationale, reasons, evidence— what proven evidence exists?
4. Questioning viewpoints and perspectives—what other perspectives exist?

5. Probing implications and consequences—what does this mean, what is the significance, and how does it connect to other information?
6. Questions about the question—why is this question important?

To check the veracity of this statement, you might ask:

- What exactly is being said, and why does it matter?
- What is that statement based on?
- What makes you think it is true? Where's the evidence for it?
- Who might have this perspective, and why? What might be the opposing perspective? Why is that?
- What does this mean for Spanish history as a whole? Are all history textbooks incorrect? What else will be affected by this knowledge?
- Why do you think I might be asking you about this?

What about using the Socratic questions for deeper understanding of a topic, such as the biology of the brain? Actually, the questions don't change—all six of the above questions can be used in the same why to more deeply understand brain structures. You'll learn, you'll poke holes, and you'll understand. Isn't that what this whole thing is all about?

There is one more framework to helping you become a question master, and it's called *Bloom's Taxonomy*. It was created by Benjamin Bloom in 1956 (though updated in 2001) as a way to measure the academic performance of college students. It has since been a staple in academic institutions to be a framework for crafting lessons that ensure a thorough comprehension in students. For our purposes, it will help us interact with information better and more actively.

It essentially states that for the highest level of understanding, there are six levels we must be able to complete. Most people will never make it through all the levels in the taxonomy, so don't let yourself fall victim to that fate.

The current taxonomy's levels are, from lowest level to highest level of understanding:

- **Remember.** Retrieving, recognizing, and recalling relevant knowledge from long-term memory.
- **Understand.** Constructing meaning from oral, written, and graphic messages through interpreting, exemplifying, classifying, summarizing, inferring, comparing, and explaining.
- **Apply.** Carrying out or using a procedure for executing or implementing.
- **Analyze.** Breaking material into constituent parts, determining how the parts relate to one another and to an overall structure or purpose through differentiating, organizing, and attributing.
- **Evaluate.** Making judgments based on criteria and standards through checking and critiquing.
- **Create.** Putting elements together to form a coherent or functional whole; reorganizing elements into a new

pattern or structure through generating, planning, or producing.

Once you hit the top level of "create," then you can be considered to have a deep grasp on a subject of skill. Without advancing through each level of the taxonomy, you can't adequately perform the next levels.

Before you can **understand** a concept, you must **remember** it. To **apply** a concept, you must first **understand** it. In order to **evaluate** a process, you must have **analyzed** it. To **create** an accurate conclusion, you must have completed a thorough **evaluation**.

Strategic questions stemming from the focus of each level can help you check your own knowledge, and the following graphic from flickr user *enokson* is illuminating as to the power of questions.

3 Application *Use of facts, rules, and principles*	apply compute conclude construct	demonstrate determine draw find out	give an example illustrate make operate	show solve state a rul operate... use
	How is ____ an example of ____? How is ____ related to ____? Why is ____ significant?		Do you know of another instance whe... Could this have happened in ____?	
4 Analysis *Separating a whole into component parts*	analyze categorize classify compare	contrast debate deduct determine the factors	diagram differentiate dissect distinguish	examine infer specify
	What are the parts or features of ____? Classify ____ according to ____. Outline/diagram/web/map ____.		How does ____ compare/contrast wit... What evidence can you present for __	
5 Synthesis *Combining ideas to form a new whole*	change combine compose construct create design	find an unusual way formulate generate invent originate plan	predict pretend produce rearrange reconstruct reorganize	revise suggest suppose visualize write
	What would you predict/infer from ____? What ideas can you add to ____? How would you create/design a new ____?		What solutions would you suggest fo... What might happen if you combined . with ____?	
6 Evaluation *Developing opinions, judgements, or decisions*	appraise choose compare conclude	decide defend evaluate give your opinion	judge justify prioritize rank	rate select support value
	Do you agree that ____? Explain. What do you think about ____? What is most important?		Prioritize ____ according to ____? How would you decide about ____? What criteria would you use to asses...	

Takeaways:

- After understanding the four cardinal aspects of effectively stuffing your brain full of information, we have a few tactics to support them.
- We must manage our attention spans and overall level of energy. The brain is a muscle, and sometimes not a very resilient or strong one at that. We get tired and distracted quite easily. Just like with spaced repetition, we must take

this into account and plan around it. One of the most effective ways is to use the Pomodoro Technique, which creates periods of twenty-five minutes of working, followed by five minutes of relaxing. The ideal outcome is to chain four of these periods together. If you "graduate" from this, you can dive into fifty minutes of working, followed by ten minutes of relaxing, or even the 60-60-30 method, which is a period of fifty minutes on, ten minutes off, fifty minutes on, and forty minutes off.

- Memory and learning are context dependent. This means that our physical environment and location are also encoded as part of a memory—after all, to the brain, information is information no matter if it comes from a textbook or the smell of a bakery. We should take advantage of this and change locations when we are learning and memorizing. Think of this as creating a wider set of hooks for which information can remain in the brain.

- Construct vivid imagery to give your memory what it wants. We are not programmed to remember boring things; in fact, we are wired to remember that which is notable and vivid. Thus, during the process of learning and memorizing, take a boring piece of information and go through the exercise and effort of dreaming up vivid imagery for it. Draw or doodle it, even. We should also utilize vivid imagery in creating stories to help memorization. Thirty percent of our brains are devoted to visual imagery, so you can see why this would be effective.

- Finally, become a question master. Information and comprehension will not present itself to you; most often, you will have to take it into your own hands. Questions will take a flat piece of information and turn it into a living, three-dimensional piece of knowledge that interacts with the world at large. That is the reality of any fact or piece of information; it has a story that we are usually overlooking. To ask a question is to see a subject, identify what you don't know, and also be open to the fact that your entire understanding could be wrong. Meaningful learning only occurs when you understand what surrounds information, such as the process and context.

- Questions can take the form of Socratic questions, which are a set of six questions that force a closer look at assumptions and underlying beliefs. Questions can also take cues from Bloom's Taxonomy, which help you analyze and evaluate information.

Chapter 4. Navigating Obstacles and Failure

Even with the best techniques and a well-honed plan for learning, it can be challenging to learn new things when you have to be both the student and teacher. This isn't because of the material itself; the techniques we've covered really can help you master and overcome any difficulty you'll find there. No, the real challenge is overcoming our own self-doubt, anxiety, and the universal tendency we have to be easily discouraged.

In this chapter, you'll find tips to help you overcome the thoughts and emotions that hold you back. We will learn to beat our own barriers that lead us to self-sabotage. In the first chapter, we saw that disempowering myths held us back out of a lack of belief. Our mental state, emotions, and inner voice telling us we can't do it are far more damaging than any archenemy could be. If these elements can affect you so much in learning, it's almost frightening to imagine how much impact they have on how you live your life.

The Procrastination Cycle

The first obstacle we will inevitably face is our overwhelming urge to procrastinate and push things off until tomorrow, later, or some other time when we *feel like it*.

To effectively battle it, we must understand the cycle in which it resides and keeps us from our textbooks, notes, or lectures.

In some ways, the existence of a cycle is a relief because it means that beating procrastination isn't so much about reaching deep inside yourself and relying on your guts to get the job done (although sometimes that part cannot be avoided). It's actually about understanding the cycle of laziness and disrupting it before you get sucked into it.

It's the equivalent of understanding how to use a certain physics equation to solve a problem versus trying to solve the problem differently each time and sometimes just trying out twenty different possibilities. When you know what you're looking for, you're going to be far more effective. In practical terms, this means that doing what you need to do will be much less of a struggle in the end.

There are five main phases of the cycle that explain why you tend to keep sitting on your butt even though you know you shouldn't be. It further explains how you justify sitting on your butt and even how you'll probably sit on your butt even more decisively the next time. We can follow along with an example of reading a textbook.

1. **Unhelpful assumptions or made-up rules**: "Life is short, so I should enjoy it and not spend my precious time reading

that boring textbook! Textbooks are only for when professors are lazy, anyway."

2. **Increasing discomfort**: "I'd rather not read the textbook. It's boring and uncomfortable. I know I have class in two hours, but it can wait."

3. **Excuses for procrastination to decrease psychological discomfort**: "It's perfectly reasonable for me not to read the textbook. It's so hot. I need to cool down first and not melt. I'm pretty sure everyone else in my class is in the same boat, and no one will have read it."

4. **Avoidance activities to decrease psychological discomfort**: "I will clean the bathroom instead. I'm still productive! I'll also arrange my desk. Lots of things getting done today. I did pretty well today, all things considered. What textbook?"

5. **Negative and positive consequences**: "Ah, I feel better about myself now. Cleanliness all around. Oh, wait. I still need to read that textbook, and class time is getting closer and closer . . ."

Which brings us full circle: the textbook is not read, and your assumptions remain the same if not reinforced, only this time, there's even more discomfort that you want to avoid immediately. And so it goes on. Once you're in the cycle, it's hard to get over the increasing inertia keeping you from getting the task done.

Let's take a look at each of the phases individually. We'll start right from the top; this is where you are either failing to start a task or to complete a task already underway. You know you should do these things and they are in your best interest. However, you've already made the decision against self-discipline, so what goes through your mind?

Unhelpful Assumptions or Made-Up Rules

If you feel like you don't want to start or follow through with something, it's not due to simple laziness or "I don't feel like it right now." It's about the beliefs and assumptions that underlie these feelings. What are some of these unhelpful assumptions or made-up rules?

My life should be about seeking pleasure, having fun, and enjoying myself. Anything that conflicts with that shouldn't be allowed. We all fall into this at one time or another. Pleasure-seeking is where you feel that life is too short to pass up something fun, interesting, or pleasant in favor of things that may seem boring or hard. Fun is the priority! At the very least, you believe that the current short-term pleasure is more important than a long-term payoff.

This is the true meaning of "I don't feel like it right now"—you are actually saying, "I want to do something more pleasurable than that right now."

I need X, Y, or Z to get to work, and if they are not present, I am excused. Sometimes you just can't muster up the energy to do something. You may feel tired, stressed, depressed, or unmotivated, and you use that as your "reason" for not getting things done. You have to be "ready." You need X, Y, and Z to start properly. You have to be *in the mood*. All these so-called requirements were conjured by you; none of them actually reflect reality.

I probably won't do it right, so I just won't do it at all. You may fall into the assumption that you must do things perfectly every time or else it will be labeled a failure. This is a fear of failure and rejection, and it also involves a lack of self-confidence. You don't want others to think less of you. And how do you ensure that neither of these things happen? You don't do it. You don't start it, and you don't finish it. There won't be failure or disappointment because you don't allow the opportunity for judgment.

If you feel that you need to do something that goes against your beliefs, you will only do it when absolutely necessary. This is a reality of human behavior, as is the fact that these beliefs are usually subconscious. So what happens if you are told to do household chores but you possess the first two beliefs of "fun comes first" and "I need perfect conditions"? You'll have fun first and then wait for a large set of preconditions, and the chores will go undone. The *rest* of the cycle is what *keeps* them undone.

Increasing Discomfort

When you are procrastinating, you're not totally unaware of what you need to do, and thus tension and discomfort will be created. Knowing you are being naughty does not promote good feelings.

You will have a range of emotions, all of which are uncomfortable: anger, boredom, frustration, exhaustion, resentment, anxiety, embarrassment, fear, or despair. The end result is that we are in an agitated state, and *we don't like feeling that way*. Something will need to change. Think of it this way: your brain doesn't want you to stay in a state of psychological discomfort— it's like standing on the bow of a sinking ship—so it deals with it the only way it knows how through the next two phases.

(Additionally, if the source of this discomfort is anything having to do with reading that darned textbook, that means you're going to avoid it like the black plague.)

Making Excuses

Excuses are the first way to make yourself feel better when you are ducking responsibility. You know you should do something, but you don't want to. Does this mean you're just lazy, tired, or entitled to no action? *Of course not.*

Admitting those would cause even more discomfort and tension than you already feel. So you construct excuses to remain the good guy or even the victim in your situation—or at least not the bad guy. Now that's a comforting thought. What would you say to make your lack of action acceptable?

"I don't want to miss out on that party tonight. I'll do it tomorrow."

"I'm just too tired tonight. I'll start working on that goal later."

"I'll do a better job on that project when I'm in the mood to work on it."

"I don't have everything I need to finish the job, so I can't start now."

"I'll do it right after I finish this other task."

Now, if you uttered these to someone else, they might reply with a raised eyebrow and a "Really . . .?" The problem is, these excuses are ones that you tell yourself. And you've probably used them so frequently in your life that the lines between your excuses and reality have blurred. You become unable to discern or tell the truth, and you unknowingly start to disempower yourself.

And while you're busy convincing yourself that these excuses are real and legitimate, you are smoothly transitioning into the next phase in the cycle: avoidance activities.

Avoidance Activities

Avoidance activities are the culmination of alleviating your discomfort and wanting to feel like you aren't simply being lazy. The internal dialogue goes something like this: "I'm sufficiently justified in not reading the textbook, but why do I still feel lousy about myself? I should *do* something . . ." Excuses on their own may not be enough, so you figure some action is still needed to lessen the discomfort and tension.

And so you act, though it's never what you should be doing in the first place. Typically, there are two types of avoidance activities. First, there are activities that simply distract you from the discomfort of choosing not to exercise your self-discipline or violate a belief or assumption. Out of sight, out of mind, and the discomfort is destroyed by going for ice cream or to a new superhero movie. This is distraction to the point of denial.

Second, there are activities that make you feel productive in some other way than the task at hand. For instance, if you work from home and are putting off a project, you will never have a cleaner bathroom than when real tasks are to be avoided. You might do an "easier" or lower-priority task. These avoidance activities allow you to say, "Well, at least I did something and wasn't totally unproductive with my time!" A fitting term for these activities is *productive procrastination*.

These activities do help you feel better about yourself in the short-term, but they don't move you any closer to where you should be, and make the cycle harder to break.

Negative and Positive Consequences

Avoiding is an art. But when you avoid responsibilities, there are always consequences. Somewhere, something is slipping through the cracks. The negative consequences are more obvious. They can include increased discomfort, guilt, anxiety, and shame. You know you're not achieving (or taking steps to achieve) your goal, and this just makes you feel worse.

Another negative consequence is having increased demands on you. Your work may accumulate, leaving you to have to do the original task plus the additional compensatory work. And depending on the nature of the task, avoidance may lead to a consequence of punishment or loss. That punishment/loss may be in the form of repercussions at work, a missed opportunity, or failing to meet a goal. The chores go undone, and your lawn gets so out of control that you start to find small, vicious woodland animals in it.

Other negative consequences are related to this very cycle, where your unhelpful or incorrect assumptions or beliefs remain unchallenged, you become overly effective at making excuses for yourself, and your tolerance for psychological discomfort shrinks even more. These all perpetuate the cycle even worse.

Any positive consequences are illusory. You may actually feel better because you are sticking to your unhelpful assumptions. And you will probably get some enjoyment from your procrastination activities. They may be positive in that they feel good in the moment, but they are temporary at best. It's like shutting your eyes to avoid the bright headlights of a truck barreling toward you—you are just setting yourself up for failure in the long term. It's self-sabotage.

Both sets of consequences contribute to furthering the cycle. Negative consequences make you want to continue avoiding certain tasks, while positive consequences inject just enough short-term pleasure to disguise what's really happening. And they both lead you right back to the initial problem of sitting on your butt.

You can now see how this can become a vicious cycle. The more you subscribe to one or more of the unhelpful assumptions, the greater your discomfort. With increasing discomfort, you start to make excuses to avoid. The more you avoid, the more you *want* to avoid it due to both the negative and positive consequences. And you start back in with the unhelpful assumptions—probably strengthened for the worst at this point.

Unfortunately, self-awareness is not a strong point for humans. But trying to acknowledge and buttress these entry points into the cycle of procrastination can help you succeed.

Academic Buoyancy

The concept of *academic buoyancy* is the second key to overcoming our own internal obstacles to learning.

Learning is bound to be difficult, even for those with supposed innate intelligence. Nothing comes easy, at least not at the levels of mastery we are aiming for. And yet, so many people take themselves out of the running by giving up at the first sign of hardship.

People who *don't* give up when they're faced with learning challenges are said to have *academic buoyancy*. Like intelligence, this isn't an inborn characteristic that some are born with, but rather a set of skills that can be learned and habits that can be cultivated to result in the ability to push past challenges and keep learning.

Confidence is just one element of academic buoyancy, but confidence alone is what allows us to overcome our fears and anxieties. In the first chapter, we discussed how confidence can unlock your lack of motivation. Imagine how much more empowered you would feel with the hardships of learning if you could embody every element.

Researchers from the University of Sydney and the University of Oxford have identified five C's that, if developed, will result in academic buoyancy. These five C's are *composure, confidence, coordination, commitment, and control*. They are not specific to learning, but they are traits that certainly harm it.

It will be apparent why they are important to overcoming obstacles associated with learning—most of them are truly not about the content or information itself. Rather, most obstacles have to do with our mindset toward it; our belief and sense of perseverance ends up being what separates most learners at the end of the day. Their influence is far, far greater than any of the techniques in this book. Is this to say that where there is a will, there is a way? Yes—learning in large part depends on how you feel about it, and the rest is just about saving time and working smarter.

Composure is the ability to manage and minimize anxiety. When learners feel anxious while engaging in their studies, it's usually because we're afraid of being ashamed and embarrassed. What if people find out we're trying to learn something, and expect us to display our knowledge? What if we fail completely when this happens? *What if we fail?* The fear can be paralyzing.

When people can't manage their anxiety, they are weighed down by their fear and crippled by the tension it produces in their bodies. In the worst cases, worries overcome the thoughts of the learner, preventing the student from focusing on and understanding new information. But there's good news: those fears are entirely baseless.

As anxiety is largely based on the fear of failure, we must directly address that. When we think about fear, we think about the worst-case scenario. Whatever we "fail" at, we imagine the world ending as a direct result. This is known as catastrophization, and it occurs whenever you ignore the realistic consequences and jump to drastic measures.

This is conquered by managing your self-talk. Acknowledge that negative things may happen, but that many of your thoughts may be irrational and fiction. Consider the alternative explanations and outcomes.

If you find yourself worrying, counter that worry with optimism. If you berate yourself for a mistake, remind yourself that it's a learning opportunity and that you'll do better next time. Any negative thought can be successfully and honestly countered by positive, encouraging, forgiving, and accepting alternatives. With time, the brain comes to accept these retorts as more valid than the negative, fearful thoughts. If anxiety is a problem for you, be persistent. This bugaboo really can be beaten. You can gain the composure you need to be academically buoyant.

Confidence, also called self-efficacy, is the belief that you are able to perform a specific task. When we lack confidence, we are certain we can't successfully accomplish a goal. We talk ourselves down, insult ourselves, and belittle any progress we make. When this happens, we often give up on our goal early before we can prove to ourselves and others that we're a failure. The trouble is that giving up is failing too; it can be satisfying to confirm these negative beliefs about ourselves, but it's far more satisfying—and less stressful—to set our doubts aside and actually reach our goals.

If you're ready to improve your confidence, there are two main techniques to employ. The first, as we saw in the section on composure, is self-talk. When your brain tells you that you're a failure or that a subject is too hard for you to learn, counter that thought with an assertion that you're going to keep studying, and with time and effort, you will succeed. If you keep countering these thoughts, they really will fade in time.

The second method is more concrete: goal-setting. We gain confidence naturally when we accomplish tasks. When we have a track record of success, it becomes harder and harder to believe our doubts have any credibility. The fastest way to do this is to create daily, or even hourly, study goals, and to watch yourself meet them over and over again. When this happens, congratulate yourself! Each goal you reach gets you one step closer to your ultimate goal of skill mastery. More than that, each goal you reach demonstrates that you have the skill and fortitude to reach the goals you set for yourself. It's a sign that your confidence is real and legitimate.

Coordination is your ability to plan and manage your time effectively. When people fail to do this, they often fall prey to *The Planning Fallacy*. This fallacy points out that people are poor at determining how long tasks take to complete. As a general rule, we presume tasks will take less time than they actually need to complete. Worse, when we presume things won't take very much time, we often put those tasks off, because we feel like we have plenty of time to get them done. This is usually untrue, and then we find ourselves with late assignments and failed work tasks.

Several steps can be taken to eliminate this problem. Minimizing distractions in your work area is a great way to start. Turn off your phone, close your door, and tell friends or family that you're busy and not to be disturbed. You should invariably do this soon after you gain a new task to complete or subject to study. Putting things off leads to being late, while doing them immediately takes advantage of all the time you have. Lastly, it's best to do the longest, most difficult task first. Leaving it for last will produce a false sense of security and may lead to your work being incomplete at the time it's due. Getting it out of the way does the opposite, setting you up for easier tasks and an early finish.

Commitment, also called grit, is a combination of passion and persistence that can be nurtured to help you reach your goals. It's easy to study for a day or a week, but attempts to build new habits often fail. When we do, we find ourselves listlessly settling into the couch to watch another movie or television show, without putting any more effort into bettering ourselves. This keeps us in the same life situation, wasting precious time, when we could be using those same hours to improve ourselves and our circumstances.

As in the previous two categories, self-talk can be a useful tool in bolstering commitment. Talking yourself into doing things and ensuring yourself that you can make it to the end are useful tools. Having others support you in a similar way and encourage you to study when you're flagging can bolster your sense of personal responsibility and keep you trucking along even when your energy is waning.

Finally, understanding what you are sacrificing and committing for can be powerful. Without a sense of how we stand to benefit, or what pain we will clearly avoid, we can sometimes lose motivation. What dreams does this information help you attain? What hardships and difficulties will be removed once you master this information? Keep these in mind and know that you are working for something greater than the current moment of discomfort.

Finally, **control**. We have to feel like we can control our fates. There are multiple aspects of this. First, we should feel that we have the ability and capacity to achieve the learning outcomes we want. Lacking this makes us feel like we are in motion just for motion's sake, never getting closer to the end goal. We covered this in an earlier chapter, but there is no real thing as innate intelligence. Well, there is, but it doesn't really affect ninety-nine percent of us in the middle of the bell curve. Understand that with hard work, the result you want is possible, and that struggles are an unavoidable part of the process. Discomfort should be the expectation, not the exception.

Second, we should feel a sense of ownership over our learning process. When we have a sense of control in our work, we feel personal responsibility, or a sense of ownership, that propels us to do our best and keep working in the face of setbacks. When we don't have that, working and studying can seem futile, like a waste of time. We will simply feel that we are being told what to do, and this is adding insult to injury.

This can be addressed by proactively making sure of what your goals are and tailoring your everyday work to reach it. Take your fate into your own hands and create your own plan. You always have the choice to float toward other people's expectations, goals, and plans, or create a personalized set for yourself to follow.

Learning itself is not a difficult task. But missing any of these academic buoyancy elements will simply set you up for failure. They are more of prerequisites to effective learning than tactics in themselves.

Academic buoyancy is perhaps better framed as *resilience*: the ability to adapt to stressful situations. More resilient people are able to "roll with the punches" and adapt to adversity without lasting difficulties; less resilient people have a harder time with stress and life changes, both major and minor. It's been found that those who deal with minor stresses more easily can also manage major crises with greater ease, so resilience has its benefits for daily life as well as for the rare major catastrophe.

Psychologist Susan Kobasa noted three elements to resilience: (1) looking at difficulties as a challenge, (2) committing to achieving a goal no matter what, and (3) limiting their efforts and even concerns only to factors that they have control over.

Another psychologist named Martin Seligman noted three different elements of resilience: (1) seeing negative events as temporary and limited, (2) not letting negative events define them or their perspective, and (3) not overly blaming or denigrating themselves for negative events.

His general theme appears to be letting negativity pass as temporary events and not being indicative of personal shortcomings.

It's clear how any of those six resilience factors can play a role in achieving the learning goals we want. It's simply about how you bounce back from failure. Failure is a part of life, and it's what we do after the fact that determines our character and, ultimately, success in life.

Productive Failure

In most situations, we tie accomplishment with success: winning, positive outcomes, and finding solutions. But in learning, a key component in achievement is *failing*.

Productive failure is an idea identified by Manu Kapur, a researcher at the National Institute of Education in Singapore. The philosophy builds on the learning paradox, wherein *not* arriving at the desired effect is as valuable as prevailing, if not more. This is not the emotional impact, rather, the neurological impact.

Kapur stated that the accepted model of instilling knowledge—giving students structure and guidance early and continuing support until the students can get it on their own—might not be the best way to actually promote learning. Although that model intuitively makes sense, according to Kapur, it's best to let students flounder by themselves without outside help.

Kapur conducted a trial with two groups of students. In one group, students were given a set of problems with full instructional support from teachers on-site. The second group was given the same problems but received no teacher help whatsoever. Instead, the second group of students had to collaborate to find the solutions.

The supported group was able to solve the problems correctly, while the group left to itself was not. But without instructional support, this second group was forced to do deeper dives into the problems by working together. They generated ideas about the nature of the problems and speculated on what potential solutions might look like.

They tried to understand the root of the problems and what methods were available to solve them. Multiple solutions, approaches, and angles were investigated that ended up providing a three-dimensional understanding of the problems.

The two groups were then tested on what they had just learned, and the results weren't even close. The group without teacher assistance *significantly outperformed* the other group. The group that did not solve the problems discovered what Kapur deemed a "hidden efficacy" in failure: they nurtured a deeper understanding of the structure of the problems through group investigation and process.

The second group may not have solved the problem itself, but they learned more about the aspects of the problem. Going forward, when those students encounter a new problem on another test, they were able to use the knowledge they generated through their trial more effectively than the passive recipients of an instructor's expertise.

Consequently, Kapur asserted that the important parts of the second group's process were their miscues, mistakes, and fumbling. When that group made the active effort to learn by themselves, they retained more knowledge needed for future problems.

Three conditions, Kapur said, make productive failure an effective process:

- Choose problems that "challenge but do not frustrate."

- Give learners the chance to explain and elaborate their processes.

- Allow learners to compare and contrast good and bad solutions.

Struggling with something is a positive condition to learning, though it requires discipline and a sense of delayed gratification. This runs counter to our instincts. How can we, so to speak, let failing work for us?

Chances are you'll come across a moment or two of defeat in your process, along with the temptation to give up. You may even sense this before you start, which can lead to crippling anxiety that can hover over your work.

Expect but don't succumb to frustration.

Anticipating frustration in advance is just good planning—but you also have to plan how to deal with it. Sketch out a plan or idea on how to alleviate frustration when it happens—most often, this will be taking a break from the situation to recharge and getting some momentary distance from the problem. Quite often, the mere act of pausing allows for objectivity to seep in, letting you see the hang-up more clearly. But in any case, it will abate the most immediate anxieties you're feeling and give you the chance to approach the issue from a more relaxed frame of mind.

It's a matter of being comfortable with a state of mental discomfort and confusion. This can be akin to juggling ten balls in the air at once and not being sure when you can place them down.

Learning mode is different from results mode, and they have entirely different measures of success. When you want to learn, you are just looking for an increase in knowledge—*any* increase is successful learning. Reframe your expectations to make the learning as important as the result—*more* important, if possible.

Explicit and static knowledge, such as facts and dates, don't necessarily benefit from this. They don't need to. But transmitting deep and layered comprehension cannot just be plugged into the brain. It must be manipulated and applied, and failure is inherent in that process. In a way, failures function similarly to the types of quesitons we discussed in an earlier chapter, where they slowly allow you to triangulate knowledge and understanding based on what's *not* working and what's *not* true.

In the end, failure acts as a blueprint for our next steps. It is a test run that didn't go as planned and thus allows you to rectify pinpointed matters for the future.

For example, let's say you're planting a vegetable garden, noting the steps and techniques you use along the way, and when it's time to harvest, some of your plants don't come out the way they are supposed to. Is it because you used the wrong soil? Use your resources to find *why* that soil was wrong and what it needs to look like. Was the failed plant too close to another? Learn techniques for maximizing placement within a small space.

Hidden in all of this is the fact that living to avoid failure, even in just learning, leads to a very different results than someone who actively seeks success. One approach wants to limit exposure and risk, while the other is focused on the end goal no matter the cost. Failure doesn't have to be your friend, but it *will* be your occasional companion, like it or not. With that in mind, it probably makes more sense to embody the approach that is about taking more risk.

Inspiration Through Failure

But wait, there's one more point on the concept of failure and how it can actually help you to your learning goals.

A study by Professor Xiaodong Lin-Siegler at Teachers College discovered that learning about the failures and struggles of important historical figures and scientific trailblazers is an important, often overlooked, aspect of student success. It provides a more accurate perspective and imparts a sense of realistic expectations and the presence of failure in everyone's life story.

Often, textbooks and learning resources only mention the successes of the people they profile, leading the readers and viewers to believe that these men and women were insurpassably great. This is actually damaging because it sets our expectations to unrealistic heights. If you only read about success, then how should you deal with failure? If it seems like everyone who is successful has never hit a significant roadblock, what does it say about you once you hit one? It's not part of the narrative, which means you are not on the path to your goals.

Most people, even people who accomplish great things, don't begin their paths through life with the belief that they'll change the world with their discoveries, inventions, and tactics. Most people, even great people, are just trying to get through the day—whether they have grand plans or not. Each moment, even moments spent planning and working toward the future, must be lived in a human way. When people reach greatness, it's always with a string of struggles and failures they've overcome and surpassed strewn behind them. The greater the success often represents the greater the number of failures. But our books and videos, when they fail to demonstrate this, often give the opposite impression.

"When kids just think Einstein is a genius, then they believe they can never measure up to him," Lin-Siegler said. "Many kids don't know that all successes require a long journey with many failures along the way."

In Lin-Sieglar's study, groups of students were told to read different accounts of famous scientists' lives. One group read traditional textbook descriptions of their accomplishments. Another group read stories about their personal and intellectual struggles, including Einstein's need to flee from Nazi Germany and Curie's need to persist through dozens of failed experiments before discovering anything worthwhile.

The group of students who read about the struggles these geniuses faced and overcame were much more likely to believe that they were just people like themselves, while those students who read the traditional description focusing on the scientists' accomplishments attributed their success to unique, innate talent that they couldn't hope to replicate themselves.

The students who understood that successful scientists—geniuses—were just people like them who kept working and trying through their failures and struggles had better grades at the end of the term. By learning about the struggles and failures of great people, these students learned that their own struggles and failures could be stepping stones on the way to phenomenal success.

By contrast, students who didn't learn about the failures and struggles of successful people were inclined to believe that their struggles indicated their own stupidity; they believed that because they weren't as successful as their heroes immediately, that they never would be, as it never occurred to them that great people also struggled and failed on their pathway to success.

The important lesson here is that everyone is human and everyone fails. Even incredibly talented people who accomplish great things fail. The most successful people are the ones who've failed the most times, and the most often—not the ones who are the smartest or most innately intelligent. The only difference between them and the people who don't make it are that they kept trying and working even when times were tough.

If you see life as a numbers game, then the value of embracing failure becomes instantly clear. For instance, to succeed five times, perhaps there must be one hundred attempts. Fifty will fail on the first tier, twenty-five more will fail on the second tier, ten more will fail on the third tier, five more will fail on the fourth tier, and five more will fail right before the finish line. Failure is a statistical inevitability.

You may not want to be a trailblazer, a great scientist, or an insanely successful businessman. You might just want to learn a new hobby or do a little better at work. But whatever your goal, it's vital to remember that failure isn't an indication that you aren't smart enough or skilled enough to succeed. It just means you have to keep trying, like all the successful people before you have done.

If you must engage in comparisons, don't compare yourself to people who are held up as archetypes in textbooks. Only compare yourself to the past version of yourself, as that is the only measure that matters.

Takeaways:

- Learning might be simple most of the time, but it is rarely easy. Often, we are starting from ground zero and struggling through the associated growing pains. It may be a while until we reach a point of epiphany or even reach a level of rudimentary understanding. Most of the obstacles we encounter come from ourselves. That's if we ever get off the couch and crack open our textbooks and attend class in the first place!

- The first obstacle we will always have to battle is procrastination and a lack of self-discipline. After all, who wants to engage in something that is usually uncomfortable and difficult? There is a self-perpetuating cycle of psychological procrastination that we must break, as opposed to just summoning a massive amount of willpower every day. The cycle is: unhelpful assumptions or made-up rules, increasing discomfort, excuses to decrease psychological discomfort, avoidance activities to decrease psychological discomfort, and negative and positive consequences. Analyze the steps of the cycle to see where you are faltering, and you will break it.

- The second step to overcoming our internal obstacles is to understand how to be more academically buoyant. Academic buoyancy articulates five traits that either empower you toward the process of learning or cause you to give up. The traits are: composure, confidence, coordination, commitment, and control. Academic buoyancy is perhaps better framed as resilience: the ability to adapt to stressful situations.

- Now, we get to failure. We will inevitably fail. It is a statistical eventuality. But failure is actually the blueprint for success. A concept called productive failure applies specifically to learning. Struggling and twisting and turning over a concept or theory leads to greater overall understanding and context than simply being handed the answer. Anticipate frustration but don't succumb to it, as it will turn out better in the long run. This may not make you feel better, but it will make you learn better.

- Finally, we may need to readjust our expectations regarding success and learning. Our ideas of the path to success are severely skewed by how the people themselves are presented. Studies showed that digging into the failures and detours of famously successful people greatly increased the resiliency of students. In a sense, success is a game of numbers, where you must attempt a certain amount of times (with corresponding failures) to even put yourself in a position to succeed.

Summary Guide

Chapter 1: A Self-Learning Plan

- The process of self-learning is deceptively simple—that is, when you strip away all the myths surrounding it, usually amounting to prerequisites to achieve your goals.
- The myths will usually revolve around the concept of innate intelligence determining your potential, certain learning styles being necessary, certain motivations being important, or a certain predetermined rate of progress based on duration of time. These are harmful and disempowering because they tell you that you can't.
- There are no real requirements to learning other than a willingness and a dash of self-discipline. But what is massively helpful in challenging that willingness and self-discipline is a set of two plans: a macro and micro plan. The

macro plan has to do with the reasons you are going to devote your time to learning something, where the micro plan has to do with the actual activities you should engage in on a daily basis. The former ensures that you end up at a goal that you desire, while the latter ensures that you achieve that goal.

Chapter 2: The Four Pillars to Self-Learning

- In the first chapter, we introduced the notion that there are no true requirements for effective self-learning. This eliminates most of the myths surrounding learning and how the brain functions, but that's a good thing. The only thing that is truly required is a plan to ensure that you are moving forward and achieving your learning goals.

- This chapter introduces the four elements of the *micro* plan—in other words, what we should actually be doing beyond reading, listening, and watching. The way that we interact with information is learning itself, and we must be intentional with our methods.

- The first element of our micro plan is transforming information into something personal to us. This is another extremely active way to interact with information. Most people passively absorb information as if through osmosis, but that is inefficient at best. When we simply take information or concepts and put it into our own words, we process it differently, even if only through repetition. We can do this through taking great notes with the four-step Peter method (take normal notes, summarize the notes and ask questions, connect the information to the topic at large, and then re-summarize to take context into account) or the Structured Analysis method of taking notes. Doodling and drawing also has a marked effect on better understanding, as well as being heavily related to how mind maps function. In the end, we come upon a guiding principle: when we are learning, we should aim to spend no more than fifty percent of our time consuming, and rather devote more time to processing and analyzing the new information.

- The second element of the micro plan is about combining new information and concepts with what we are already familiar with. This step may not come naturally, but thinking in analogies and creating concrete examples with the information you've gained will cement your comprehension. They both require a deeper conceptual understanding of what you've learned, and in addition, they may uncover more thorough levels of knowledge. When you are able to use analogies and examples with new information, it is a sign of mastery.

- The third element is self-testing and practicing drawing information out of your brain instead of trying to stuff information into it. This may be counterintuitive, but the more we can engage in mini tests, the better we memorize and learn. This is known as retrieval practice, as you are retrieving information. Though this is mostly done through the context of flashcards, the overarching lesson is that we must be active in our efforts. The bigger the struggle, the deeper the learning and memorization. When you force yourself to learn, well, you will learn. There is no real shortcut.

- The fourth element of the micro plan is to be stingy with your mental and physical energy. The brain is like a muscle in that it can't work all day and all night and still function well. One of the key techniques that help guard against this is spaced repetition, which implores you to focus on frequency rather than duration of learning. This has been proven to be more effective than most other conventional study schedules. In fact, there are three factors that we should be mindful of when we try to give ourselves the space for absorption to occur: intensity, frequency, and duration. We can only focus on, at best, two at a time, so make sure you are not setting yourself up for failure and burnout.

Chapter 3. Tactics for Learning

- After understanding the four cardinal aspects of effectively stuffing your brain full of information, we have a few tactics to support them.
- We must manage our attention spans and overall level of energy. The brain is a muscle, and sometimes not a very resilient or strong one at that. We get tired and distracted quite easily. Just like with spaced repetition, we must take this into account and plan around it. One of the most effective ways is to use the Pomodoro Technique, which creates periods of twenty-five minutes of working, followed by five minutes of relaxing. The ideal outcome is to chain four of these periods together. If you "graduate" from this, you can dive into fifty minutes of working, followed by ten minutes of relaxing, or even the 60-60-30 method, which is a period of fifty minutes on, ten minutes off, fifty minutes on, and forty minutes off.
- Memory and learning are context dependent. This means that our physical environment and location are also encoded as part of a memory—after all,

to the brain, information is information no matter if it comes from a textbook or the smell of a bakery. We should take advantage of this and change locations when we are learning and memorizing. Think of this as creating a wider set of hooks for which information can remain in the brain.

- Construct vivid imagery to give your memory what it wants. We are not programmed to remember boring things; in fact, we are wired to remember that which is notable and vivid. Thus, during the process of learning and memorizing, take a boring piece of information and go through the exercise and effort of dreaming up vivid imagery for it. Draw or doodle it, even. We should also utilize vivid imagery in creating stories to help memorization. Thirty percent of our brains are devoted to visual imagery, so you can see why this would be effective.

- Finally, become a question master. Information and comprehension will not present itself to you; most often, you will have to take it into your own hands.

Questions will take a flat piece of information and turn it into a living, three-dimensional piece of knowledge that interacts with the world at large. That is the reality of any fact or piece of information; it has a story that we are usually overlooking. To ask a question is to see a subject, identify what you don't know, and also be open to the fact that your entire understanding could be wrong. Meaningful learning only occurs when you understand what surrounds information, such as the process and context.

- Questions can take the form of Socratic questions, which are a set of six questions that force a closer look at assumptions and underlying beliefs. Questions can also take cues from Bloom's Taxonomy, which help you analyze and evaluate information.

Chapter 4. Navigating Obstacles and Failure

- Learning might be simple most of the time, but it is rarely easy. Often, we are starting from ground zero and struggling through the associated growing pains. It may be a while until we reach a point of epiphany or even reach a level of rudimentary understanding. Most of the obstacles we encounter come from ourselves. That's if we ever get off the couch and crack open our textbooks and attend class in the first place!

- The first obstacle we will always have to battle is procrastination and a lack of self-discipline. After all, who wants to engage in something that is usually uncomfortable and difficult? There is a self-perpetuating cycle of psychological procrastination that we must break, as opposed to just summoning a massive amount of willpower every day. The cycle is: unhelpful assumptions or made-up rules, increasing discomfort, excuses to decrease psychological discomfort, avoidance activities to decrease psychological discomfort, and negative and positive consequences. Analyze the steps of the cycle to see where you are faltering, and you will break it.

- The second step to overcoming our internal obstacles is to understand how to be more academically buoyant. Academic buoyancy articulates five traits that either empower you toward the process of learning or cause you to give up. The traits are: composure, confidence, coordination, commitment, and control. Academic buoyancy is perhaps better framed as resilience: the ability to adapt to stressful situations.

- Now, we get to failure. We will inevitably fail. It is a statistical eventuality. But failure is actually the blueprint for success. A concept called productive failure applies specifically to learning. Struggling and twisting and turning over a concept or theory leads to greater overall understanding and context than simply being handed the answer. Anticipate frustration but don't succumb to it, as it will turn out better in the long run. This may not make you feel better, but it will make you learn better.

- Finally, we may need to readjust our expectations regarding success and learning. Our ideas of the path to success are severely skewed by how the people themselves are presented. Studies showed that digging into the failures and detours of famously successful people greatly increased the resiliency of students. In a sense, success is a game of numbers, where you must attempt a certain amount of times (with corresponding failures) to even put yourself in a position to succeed.

CPSIA information can be obtained
at www.ICGtesting.com
Printed in the USA
LVHW051037180520
655841LV00007B/394